TALKING SENSE

Brian Keaney

Bill Lucas

Oxford University Press 1987

Oxford University Press, Walton Street, Oxford OX2 6DP

Oxford New York Toronto
Delhi Bombay Calcutta Madras Karachi
Petaling Jaya Singapore Hong Kong Tokyo
Nairobi Dar es Salaam Cape Town
Melbourne Auckland

and associated companies in
Beirut Berlin Ibadan Nicosia

Oxford is a trade mark of Oxford University Press

© Brian Keaney and Bill Lucas 1987

ISBN 0 19 8311583

Set by MS Filmsetting Ltd, Frome and London
Printed in Great Britain by R. J. Acford, Chichester

Contents

4   How to use this book

6   **Unit 1 Organising ideas**
8   For better or worse: *planning the future*
10 Campaign tactics: *taking decisions*
12 Bon voyage: *organising a holiday*
14 Accidents can happen: *problem solving*
16 A murder mystery: *assessing evidence*

18 **Unit 2 Playing roles**
20 Making relationships: *understanding the roles you play*
22 Making the best of yourself: *selling yourself in an interview*
24 Talking your way out of . . .: *playing different everyday roles*
26 You had me fooled: *detailed improvisation*
28 Feedback: *roles from science fiction*

30 **Unit 3 Giving opinions**
32 A programmed discussion: *structured talking*
34 Speaker's corner: *speech making exercise*
36 Developing an argument: *exercises in building up a case*
38 Terrorism: *tackling a political matter*
40 Nuclear energy: *discussing a contentious subject*

42 **Unit 4 Writing together**
44 Story-shaping: *examining myth*
46 Creating a radio play: *working from background material*
48 The Charlotte Dymond case: *turning a poem into a script*
50 News and views: *different styles of writing*
52 School with a view: *writing a booklet together*

54 **Unit 5 Investigating the media**
56 Spotting bias: *noticing points of view*
58 Playgroup politics: *images of society in children's books*
60 Television advertisements: *examining codes of practice*
62 The Royal Family in the news: *styles of coverage*
64 Presenting environmental issues: *developing your own style of presentation*

Extension activities
66 A problem-solving activity
68 Fortune telling: a planning activity
70 Role-play activities
74 In the name of the law
76 A structured talking activity
78 Developing an argument
79 Talking about issues
80 More issues: patriotism
82 One-liners
84 A working-with-stories activity
86 How to have a formal debate
88 Important discussions world wide

90 Answers
91 To the student
94 To the teacher
96 Acknowledgements

To anyone using this book

How to work in a group

Talking almost inevitably involves listening. To take part successfully in this activity, it therefore nearly always follows that you will be working in a group when you are doing oral work.

A popular approach

Here is one easily-adapted method of working with the material in this book.

The teacher introduces the topic for discussion	Small groups are organised
The groups organise themselves in ways appropriate to the tasks and start discussion	The groups are given a number of tasks
From time to time individuals or groups report on how they are getting on	As the time allotted runs out groups gather together their ideas and responses
Sometimes after discussion involving the whole group conclusions are drawn or arguments summarised	There is a plenary session in which each group reports back on its discussions to the whole group
Some kind of follow-up activity is suggested by students or the teacher	Students and teachers increasingly feel confident to comment on their achievements, on the material and on the methods of working adopted by different groups. See pages 91-95

Some common questions answered

What kind of group?

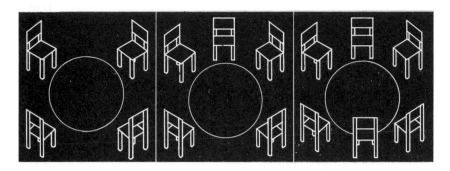

The size can vary from four to six or sometimes even larger.
It could be single-sex, or for some situations, a mixture of sexes may help.
You may be friends.
It may be a group whose members don't know each other well.

How do you start off?

Sometimes only after allowing a pause for thinking time.
Sometimes by *brainstorming*, i.e. contributing ideas *without any critical comment* while someone jots them down.
By giving each person in turn a chance to say something.
By allowing one person to guide or lead discussion.

How do you make sure oral work in groups is successful?

> You can't! But you can learn how to by teaching yourself some of the skills involved, in the same way as you did when learning to read or write as a younger person.

There is no single way of organising talk.
Sometimes you will still want to be very structured; sometimes freer discussion will be more helpful.
Try and adapt your approach or role to the task in hand:

For example

    listening and thinking
    chairing
    summarising
    giving opinions and ideas
    changing your mind or holding to an opinion
    making notes
    suggesting new approaches
    disagreeing politely
    reporting back

UNIT 1 ORGANISING IDEAS

Starters

Arranging a room

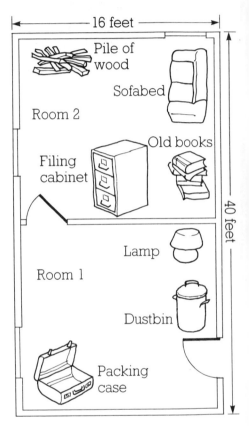

Your house has been destroyed in a fire. You and your family have been given two rooms in a large, practically empty house to use until your house can be rebuilt.

1 Study this plan of the rooms and decide what you would keep and what would be of little use to you.

2 You managed to save ten major items of furniture from the blaze. Make a list of the ten most useful items you would have hoped to save if your *own* house or flat had been burnt down.

3 **In pairs,** talk about how to arrange the two rooms to make your life as easy as possible. Draw the rooms to include the ten items saved from the fire.

Protect and survive

In 1980 the Government published a booklet with this name. Many people now see it as an unrealistic set of instructions. In it, ordinary people were asked to consider how they would survive in their homes for fourteen days after a nuclear war.

The 'five essentials for survival' listed were:
1 Drinking water
2 Food
3 Portable radio and spare batteries
4 Tin opener, bottle opener, cutlery and crockery
5 Warm clothing

1 In a group, brainstorm a list of all the other items you would consider essential.
2 Agree on the ten most important items.
3 Draw up a list of five reasons why you:
   either think it sensible to plan for surviving a nuclear war
   or think it foolish to suggest that survival is possible after nuclear war.

Washday

1 **In pairs,** read these instructions which are taken from the side of a packet of washing powder. Are they easy to understand or difficult?

2 Do you know what acrylics, acetates and triacetates are?

3 Where else do you see the symbols printed on the left of the instructions?

4 What does 'colour-fast' mean? If you did not know whether something made of cotton was colour-fast or not, what would be the best thing to do?

5 How many separate programs would you have to use to wash the following clothes?

1 pair pyjamas, dark blue cotton
2 sheets, white cotton
15 pairs of socks, polyester/cotton
1 pillow case cover, white cotton
8 shirts, various colours, nylon
2 pullovers, wool
1 cardigan, wool
15 pairs pants, cotton/polyester
1 duvet cover, dark blue cotton
4 tee-shirts pale yellow cotton
1 pair gloves, wool

6 If you ended up with 4 green tee-shirts among your washing, what would have gone wrong?

	MACHINE	HANDWASH
1 95°C	VERY HOT TO BOIL Maximum wash	HAND-HOT 50°C OR BOIL
	Spin or wring.	
	WHITE COTTON AND LINEN ARTICLES WITHOUT SPECIAL FINISHES.	
2 60°C	HOT Maximum wash	HAND-HOT 50°C
	Spin or wring.	
	COTTON, LINEN OR VISCOSE ARTICLES WITHOUT SPECIAL FINISHES WHERE COLOURS ARE FAST AT 60°C.	
3 60°C	HOT Medium wash	HAND-HOT 50°C
	Cold rinse. Short spin or drip-dry.	
	WHITE NYLON, WHITE POLYESTER/COTTON MIXTURES.	
4 50°C	HAND-HOT Medium wash	HAND-HOT
	Cold rinse. Short spin or drip-dry.	
	COLOURED NYLON; POLYESTER; COTTON & VISCOSE ARTICLES WITH SPECIAL FINISHES; ACRYLIC/COTTON MIXTURES; COLOURED POLYESTER/COTTON MIXTURES.	
5 40°C	WARM Medium wash	WARM
	Spin or wring.	
	COTTON, LINEN OR VISCOSE ARTICLES WHERE COLOURS ARE FAST AT 40°C, BUT NOT AT 60°C.	
6 40°C	WARM Minimum wash	WARM
	Cold rinse. Short spin. Do not wring.	
	ACRYLICS; ACETATES AND TRIACETATES, INCLUDING MIXTURES WITH WOOL; POLYESTER/WOOL BLENDS.	
7 40°C	WARM Minimum wash	WARM Do not rub
	Spin. Do not hand wring.	
	WOOL, INCLUDING BLANKETS AND WOOL MIXTURES WITH COTTON OR VISCOSE; SILK.	
8 30°C	COOL Minimum wash	COOL
	Cold rinse. Short spin. Do not wring.	
	SILK AND PRINTED ACETATE FABRICS WITH COLOURS NOT FAST AT 40°C.	

Key qualities

1 Which of these qualities do you consider to be most important in
   a) a friend of the same sex
   b) a friend of the opposite sex?

Put them in order for yourself. Agree an order for your group.

loyalty	good looks	independence	intelligence
affection	taste	self-confidence	kindness
trust	sense of humour	physical agility	generosity

2 Do the same for these people:
   a) a politician
   b) a TV chat show host/ess
   c) a surgeon
   d) a missionary
   e) a pop star
   f) a youth leader

For better or worse

1 Jane and Stephen are both just eighteen years old. Yesterday they told their families that they will be getting married in a month's time. Read their families' reactions.

Jane's father: 'It's ridiculous. She's just a kid. She ought to wait a few years and look around properly.'

Jane's mother: 'Well they do say that most young marriages end up in divorce. I think they ought to get engaged and give it six months. If they still want to get married after that it's up to them.'

Jane's sister (15): 'She must be mad, getting tied down to one man already. She'll spend the rest of her life looking after babies and doing the washing up.'

Stephen's father: 'They haven't got any money. You need money to set up house. They should get engaged and start saving. When they've got enough money to put a deposit on a house, that's the time to start thinking about getting married.'

Stephen's mother: 'Well I'm all for it. They love each other and that's all that counts.'

Stephen's brother (16): 'I think they should live together for at least a year to see show they get on together. Seeing someone in the evening isn't the same as being with them all the time, every day.'

2 Which of these statements do you most agree with? Why?

3 Read the extract below from the traditional Church of England marriage-service:

> FIRST it was ordained for the procreation of children, to be brought up in the fear and nurture of the Lord and to the praise of his holy Name. Secondly it was ordained for a remedy against sin and to avoid fornication that such persons as have not the gift of continency might marry and keep themselves undefiled members of Christ's body. Thirdly it was ordained for mutual society, help and comfort that the one ought to have of the other both in prosperity and adversity.

4 **In pairs,** agree on the three reasons that the Church of England traditionally considered the most important aspects of marriage.

5 How important are these reasons nowadays? To you? To your friends? To your parents/family?

6 Make a list of three good reasons for getting married and three good reasons for not. Talk about any circumstances you can think of that might affect this decision.

7 Discuss any alternatives to getting married.

8 What things do you think are most important in making a long-term relationship work? Make a list of what the two partners ought to bring to such a relationship. Would the qualities a man should bring be any different from the qualities a woman should bring?

9 Do you think it is acceptable for men to live with men and women with women?

10 Listen to the different views of marriage expressed by *all* the groups.

Campaign tactics

Never believe in mirrors or newspapers. *John Osborne*

10.9.87

RESULTS SHOCK

Angry parents of pupils at Porterton School met last night with the headteacher, John Taylor. The meeting followed the news that an entire class had failed 'A' levels in French and German.

Mrs. Alcott of Potterton P.T.A. told our reporter that she has determined to press for the dismissal of the Head of Modern Languages.

20.3.87

BREAK UP BREAK IN

Only hours after Porterton School broke up for the Easter holidays, vandals broke into the school's audio-visual store. Computers and video recorders were smashed and obscene graffiti were daubed on the walls. This incident follows shortly on the heels of last week's expulsions for drugtaking. Police say they have not ruled out the possibility that this was reprisal action by the pupils concerned.

6.1.87

LITTER LOUTS

Residents of the Leys Estate area of the city yesterday handed a petition to their City Councillor with over a hundred signatures. Mrs Jenny Black, a pensioner, told us, 'It's disgusting. The kids from the Porterton drop their crisp packets everywhere. They throw their fag ends and other litter into our gardens. I've rung the headmaster, but he doesn't seem to care. We're really fed up. It wasn't like this when old Mrs Cox was in charge. She'd have sorted them out and no mistaking!'

11.9.87

SLANDER CAMPAIGN: EDITOR APOLOGISES

We apologise and withdraw completely an article which appeared in yesterday's *Mail* under the headline, **RESULTS SHOCK.** None of the information relating to the Porterton School's Language Department's 'A' level results was true. Information given to the newspaper was false. The newspaper regrets very much any damage done to the school's reputation, especially in the light of its recent national award. Police are investigating allegations of an organised slander campaign against the school.

13.7.87

SCHOOL IN LINE FOR NATIONAL AWARD

Porterton School is one of twenty schools from all over the country that have reached the final stage in a nationwide search for schools with the most exciting curriculums. Students at Porterton are now able to choose from a range of exciting new 'modules' for which they are awarded credits. These vary from micro-computing to forensic science, contemporary dance to practical experience of community work.

Porterton head, John Taylor, told us that he was delighted with the possibility of the school gaining national recognition.

1 Piece together all the information presented in these imaginary articles. Discuss:
   a) the picture presented in the local press of Porterton School between January and September 1987.
   b) the kind of school that you think Porterton would probably be in 'reality'.

2 Porterton has a School Council (made up of students from every group). The School Council helps to determine matters of school policy. It has recently persuaded the Head to relax uniform regulations.

The School Council is very concerned about the apparent slander campaign.

At their meeting a number of issues were discussed.

School Council Meeting: 12.9.87

Agenda

1. 'The Mail'.
2. What the public thinks, eg discipline, litter, graffiti, uniform etc.
3. Campaign to improve our image.
4. AOB.

In groups, plan a campaign to improve the image of the school. You could:
   think of ways of getting *good* news coverage
   think of ways of improving relations locally
   organise a public meeting or anything else that you consider appropriate.

Plan it *in detail*, making notes/ plans for all your activities.
Compare and evaluate the different groups' suggestions/schemes.

3 Do the same for your own school.

4 Talk about whether a school council would be a good idea for your school and, if appropriate, plan how you might set one up.

Bon voyage

1 Imagine that you are a responsible adult. You have saved up for the past twelve months and now you are taking your two children, aged 7 and 3, on holiday. You do not have much money so you have to plan this carefully. Read the details of what is available to you.

Note: Prices shown below for travel and accommodation are for adults. Children under 16 are half price; children under 4 are free. One exception to this is the airfare which is for the seat regardless of age.

Route 1 By plane	Adult return fare
Train from hometown to city	£2.50
Bus from station to airport	£1.00
Airfare...	£75.00*
Bus from airport to hotel	£1.00

*adult or child

Route 2 By train/boat	Adult return fare
Train from hometown to city	£2.50
Train/boat from city to port............	£50.00
Bus from port to resort...............	£1.00

Optional: Cabin to sleep 2 adults £20.00 each way.

Journey time

Air travel: Depart 16.00 Arrive 17.30 same day
Train/boat: Depart London 18.00 Arrive 06.00 following day

Hotel accommodation:

£12.00 per person, per night
Hotel provides breakfast only

Budget

You will need spending money and money for emergencies. You have saved £350 altogether.

2 How much would it cost to travel by train and boat, if you did not book a cabin?

3 If you did not book a cabin you and the children would have to sleep on chairs in the ship's lounge (if you were lucky enough to find three empty chairs). Would it be worth the discomfort to save the money?

4 How much would it cost to travel by air?

5 The last time you travelled by boat the seven-year-old was sea-sick. On the other hand there have been a series of plane hijackings recently. Bearing this in mind, and remembering how much money you have altogether, which method of travel would you choose?

6 The climate at the resort is hot and sunny though sometimes variable. Recently there have been freak hailstorms. Make a list of essential items you would pack in your luggage. Don't forget about the children's needs.

7 What things go to make up a really good holiday? Make a list of your top five demands from a really excellent holiday.

8 The travel agent has offered you a choice of three hotels. Read the details printed below and decide which would be the best choice.

HOTEL VESPASIA

The popular Hotel Vespasia is run by its owner, Senor Halva and has plenty of facilities for its guests to enjoy. It is a large, lively modern hotel situated away from the bustling town centre, on the main promenade directly opposite the beach. The disco is very popular with the young and the young at heart.

Amenities

* Swimming pool with adjoining children's pool
* Sun terrace surrounding the pool
* Poolside bar
* Spacious lounge bar
* Snack bar
* Dancing to live music weekly
* Discotheque
* TV lounge
* Late night pub with entertainment
* Children's play area

HOTEL GRANDE

The modern Hotel Grande is located close to a sandy beach. It has good facilities, including bars, a swimming pool, a disco and a video lounge showing films in English. There are shops, bars, cafés and night clubs in the nearby town.

Amenities

* 3 bars including "El Dorro" cellar music bar
* 2 lifts
* Garden
* Games room
* Children's play area
* Disco bar
* Swimming pool
* Children's pool
* Snack bar
* TV/Video lounge

HOTEL BELLE PARK

The Hotel Belle Park stands just 200 metres from the beach and just ten minutes walk from the town centre. This fine hotel offers a relaxed and informal atmosphere with good amenities. The restaurant overlooks the palm-fringed sun terrace and swimming pool.

Amenities

* 2 bars
* Lift
* Large garden surrounding pool area
* Games machine in bar area
* Children's play area
* Disco
* TV lounge
* Swimming pool
* Children's pool
* Pool tables, table tennis
* Tennis court
* Party & barbecue nights

Accidents can happen

1 Below are details of an accident that happened at Embleton
Green School. Mr Surridge, one of the teachers, was hit in the
face by a door. Study the diagram. Then read Mr Surridge's
accident report, the letter from Stephen Mitchell and what the
school caretaker said afterwards.

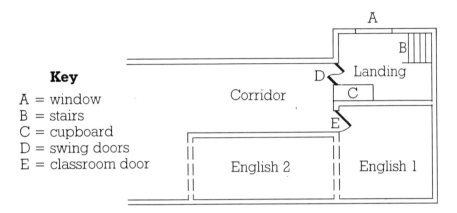

Key

A = window
B = stairs
C = cupboard
D = swing doors
E = classroom door

Accident report

I was on my way to my classroom, English 1, to teach my fourth
form. I came up the back stairs and crossed the landing. I
approached the left-hand double door and put out my hand to open
it. Just then the door swung open, hitting me in the face and
knocking me to the ground. I was taken by ambulance to the local
hospital where I received three stitches to a cut on my forehead.

Letter of apology

> *Embleton Green School*
> *2 May 1987*
>
> *Dear Mr Surridge,*
> *   I am sorry to have hit you in the face with the door. I did not do it on
> purpose. As you know the glass in the doors had been boarded up by the schoolkeeper
> so it was not possible to see if anyone was on the other side. It was really Trevor
> Howard's fault. He started chasing me down the corridor and I was trying to get
> away from him when I pushed the doors open.*
>
> *   Yours sincerely,*
>
> *   Stephen Mitchell*

What the caretaker said

'Well if you ask me it serves him right. Time and time again I've spoken to those teachers about the kids on that corridor. They let them run around like mad. That's how come there was no glass in the door. It's been smashed so many times already this term, I can't keep replacing it.'

2   Decide what you think were the causes of the accident. Make a list of the three main causes in order.

3   Mr Surridge is suing the Education Authority for compensation. They are contesting this on grounds of 'contributory negligence'. They say that it was partly Mr Surridge's fault because everybody should approach a door with proper care and attention and should stand to one side as they open it. Can you suggest how Mr Surridge might reply to this?

4   There were two signs, one at either end of the corridor, which read: *Walk in the corridor*. Do you think this was a reasonable attempt to control behaviour in the corridor? What more could have been done by the school?

5   Mr Surridge spent three hours in hospital receiving treatment. The accident happened just before the half term holiday. He had planned to go away for a few days but he spent the time resting and recovering. He has been left with a small scar just above his left eye, measuring about one centimetre across. Although he was not knocked unconscious by the blow, he was severely dazed and had to be supported to the ambulance. Taking all this into account, how much compensation would you award Mr Surridge?

6   Stephen Mitchell has been suspended from school for three days. Do you think this is a fair punishment? How would you have treated him?

7   Are there parts of your school which could be danger spots? Which areas are they and what could be done to improve them?

A murder mystery

1 Below are the details of a murder. Study the diagram and read the facts of the case.

The guest wing

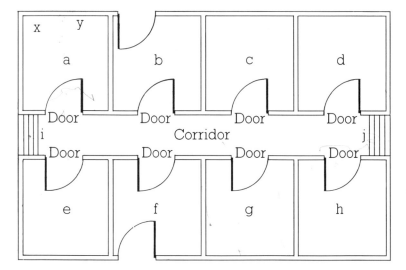

Key

a Mr Ford's bedroom
b Mr Ford's bathroom
c Mr O'Rourke's bedroom
d Shared bathroom
e Ms Delworth's bedroom
f Ms Delworth's bathroom
g Mr Svensson's bedroom
h Ms De La Roche's bedroom
i Stairs to sitting-room
j Stairs to swimming-pool
x Mr Ford's body found here
y Damp patch

Facts of the case

Hudson Ford, the multi-millionaire, was found murdered one night in February. Cries were heard coming from the bedroom and one of the servants went to investigate. He found Mr Ford dead inside. There were marks on his throat where an attempt had been made to strangle him, but the cause of death was undoubtedly a wound received from a knife found on the bed. One of the guests, Mr O'Rourke, was standing just outside the room. He said he had been for a walk but had come in because of the rain. Hearing cries, he had also gone to investigate. However the servant noticed a wet patch in Mr Ford's room behind the curtains. He quickly sent for the police and Mr O'Rourke was arrested.

2 Mark Members, the famous detective, was staying in the area. When he heard of the case he came to lend his assistance. He questioned the guests and servants, then shook each of them by the hand. Finally he turned to the police inspector. 'You've arrested the wrong person,' he said. 'The killer was...' But before you hear Mark Member's verdict, read the evidence yourself and see if you can tell who the murderer was.

Evidence

Guests

Marie Delworth – an actress from Nashville, Tennessee. Her engagement to Mr Ford was recently rumoured though neither she nor Mr Ford had confirmed this. She said that she asked the maid to run a bath. The maid did so at 11.30 p.m. She got into the bath immediately. She heard the commotion a little while later but did not come out to see what had happened because she was not dressed.

Sven Svensson – the ex-World Snooker Champion. His unusual left-handed style had taken the snooker world by storm three years ago but there were rumours that he drank too much nowadays. He had not won a match for eighteen months. He said that he had been swimming in the pool with Ms De La Roche until 11.25 p.m. Then he had gone up to his room to change. He had not heard anything unusual until the police had arrived.

Patti De La Roche – an expert in marine biology. She had been advising Ford on a film he was making called *Ten Thousand Leagues Under The Sea*. She said that she had stayed in the pool after Svensson left. She had been there when the police arrived.

Declan O'Rourke – an old friend of Mr Ford's. They had first met ten years earlier when they had been in the oil business together. O'Rourke had retired from the business because of severe rheumatoid arthritis.

Servants

Cogshill – the butler. He had been in the sitting room clearing up when he had heard cries. He knew the exact time because he had been setting the clock right. It was 11.43 p.m. He had rushed upstairs and found Mr Ford dead and Mr O'Rourke standing outside his room.

Jane Leggett – the maid. She confirmed that Ms Delworth had asked her to run a bath and that she had done so at 11.30 p.m. She added that five minutes later she had knocked on the door of Ms Delworth's bathroom to ask if there was anything else she wanted. Ms Delworth had said no, so she had continued along the corridor and down the stairs to the swimming pool intending to turn off the pool lights. She had been surprised to find Ms De La Roche still swimming. Ms De La Roche had said she would turn off the lights herself. Jane Leggett looked at her watch. It was just after 11.40 p.m. She said goodnight to Ms De La Roche and went to bed.

Mark Members examined the scene of the crime carefully. He decided that the wet patch had definitely been caused by a person standing there. He found written on the wall in Mr Ford's own blood, the letters: 'TEN'. It was clear that Mr Ford had written them himself. He ran from the door of Mr Ford's room to the top of the stairs leading to the swimming pool and timed himself. It took three minutes. He examined the murder weapon for finger prints. There were none.

3   How did Mark Member know that Declan O'Rourke was not the murderer?

4   How do you think the murderer avoided being seen by either Coghill, the butler, or Declan O'Rourke?

5   What motive do you think the murderer might have had?

UNIT 2 PLAYING ROLES

Starters

Role play

In pairs

1 Have a conversation in which one of you compliments the other person who doesn't believe anything you say.

2 Have a conversation about something important which has happened to you, but which you let slip only when pressed to do so by your partner. (Intelligent guesswork and prompting will be important here.)

3 Discuss someone you both know in a friendly and positive way.

4 Ask your partner what people think of you and vice versa. Try to be honest and helpful.

In groups

You are in a shop. Decide how old you are and why you are there. One of you should be an employee of the shop. Allow something to make all but one of you laugh. Without actually spelling it out, make it clear what is annoying you. Resolve the scene in an unusual way. You could act it out.

Building up a character

Thomasina or Thomas Scott
You are 26. You are a keep-fit fanatic. You don't smoke or drink. You eat very carefully and are generally critical of others who don't share your views. You would like to find a partner in life who thinks similarly.

Make up names and characters for these two sets of pictures. Try to go beyond the obvious ideas suggested by them.

Pensioner in bank raid

By Martin Wainwright

The Old Bailey listened spellbound yesterday to the tale of a pensioner's doomed attempt to hold hostages at a London bank and rob it of £85,000. Mrs Peggy Barlow, aged 70, of West Kensington, skipped her weekly bridge party to carry out the raid, travelling on her bus pass and armed with a perfume spray which she pretended was a gun.

She grabbed a customer at the bank and bundled her into the manager's office, pressing the perfume canister into her side in a style she had noticed on a TV film about Chicago gangsters. Then she ordered everyone to keep quiet and demanded all the money in the bank, modifying this to £85,000 after a delay which led her to shout: "Hurry up, I'm desperate!"

Mrs Barlow, who walks with the help of a stick and is a bank manager's widow herself, admitted demanding the money with menaces from Mr David Ball, manager of the National Westminster Bank in Kensington High Street.

Her counsel, Mr Brian Barker, said that the story was almost beyond belief and involved an "extraordinary aberration" brought on by threats of bankruptcy. Mrs Barlow who has two grown-up children, had debts of £70,000 and faced daily demands from creditors in the weeks before her raid.

"A younger person may have been able to take this desperate financial situation in their stride but it worried this lady so much that she turned bandit," said Mr Barker.

The court heard that Mrs Barlow had put herself in some danger, with armed police wearing bullet-proof jackets sent to the bank after staff pressed a panic button. Although her planning was sophisticated she reckoned without her hostage, Mrs Julien Watkins.

Mr Peter Doyle, prosecuting, said that Mrs Watkins had suddenly decided to have a go and had pinned Mrs Barlow to the wall with the help of the bank manager. Three policemen arrived and arrested Mrs Barlow.

From *The Guardian* 6.10.84

[The rest of the article appears on page 90.]

1 Make a list of all the things you know about Mrs Peggy Barlow's character from reading this extract.
2 **In pairs,** make up the conversation that Peggy Barlow might have had with her counsel, Mr Brian Barker.
3 **In a group,** give the speech you would have given when sentencing Mrs Barlow if you had been the judge.

Conversations

1 Decide who these people are.
2 Choose two pairs of characters and make up the conversation you think they might have had:
   a) on the telephone or **b)** at lunch or **c)** in the street.

19

Making relationships

1 Which of these people do you have relationships with in your
   daily life? Add any others that you can think of.

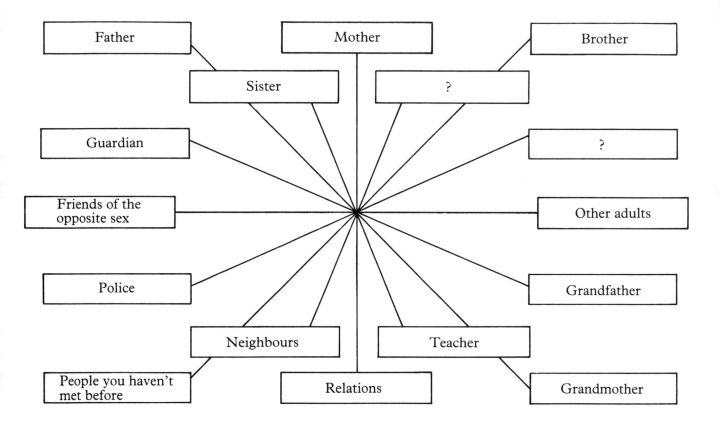

2 Make a list of the people you find
   a) most easy and
   b) most difficult to get on with.
   Compare your answers with others in the group.

3 Which people would you talk about these subjects with?
        How much money you spend on clothes
        Your feelings about sex
        Your opinions about violence on TV
        Your weaknesses
        What you really think about your family
        Your taste in music

   In your group, talk about why you can discuss certain subjects
   with certain people. Try and agree some general statements
   about this.

4 Choose one of these subjects and talk about it with someone else
   in your group. Talk for about two minutes and then swap over.

Meeting someone for the first time

5   **In pairs,** decide where you would be most likely to meet these people in the course of your normal life:
     a doctor
     a neighbour
     a girl/boyfriend
     a headteacher

6   **In pairs,** make up the kind of conversation you might have if you were meeting for the first time. Take it in turns to be yourself and to play one of the roles. Give your conversation a purpose.

Example

A: It's Mr. Jenkins, isn't it?
B: Yes.
A: Hello! I'm Elaine Yates from number 22. We moved in last week. I was wondering if you could tell me....

Saying goodbye for the last time

7   **In pairs,** make up a conversation between two friends, one of whom is moving with her/his family to another country. Make the relationship clear.

8   **In pairs,** make up a conversation in which a long-standing relationship is ended **either**

     a) angrily and bitterly
     or
     b) in a friendly but sad way.
     Decide where you met, how long you knew each other and why one of you is leaving.

9   Continue this conversation in any way you like.

The End of Something

Marjorie: What's the matter Nick?
Nick: I don't know.

(*Pause*)

Nick: There's going to be a moon, tonight.
Marjorie: I know it.
Nick: You know everything.
Marjorie: Oh, Nick, cut it out. Please, please don't be that way.
Nick: I can't help it. You do. You know everything. That's the trouble...

From a story by Ernest Hemingway

Making the best of yourself

Their little interview was like a picnic on a coral strand.
Henry James

The job interview

1   **In groups,** answer these questions about the two interviews on
    the opposite page.
    a) What do you understand by the term 'Personnel officer'?
    b) What are the six basic questions that the personnel officer
       asks both interviewees?
    c) Is there any more to being 'a good manager' than 'getting
       the best out of people', as interviewee B says? List any
       points you would add.
    d) From the personnel officer's questions, what qualities do
       you think s/he is looking for in a manager? Rank them
       according to your view of their importance.
    e) Which question does interviewee B answer best in your
       view?
    f) Choose six words to describe the qualities interviewee A
       shows in her/his interview.

2   Make a list of the six questions you would ask someone if you
    were interviewing them for these jobs:
    a) a Saturday job in a shoe shop
    b) a training place in a hair salon
    c) a place on an arts course at a university
    d) a place on a science course at a polytechnic
    e) a helper in a playgroup
    f) a training place in a car factory

3   What questions would you ask to find out about a candidate's
    a) confidence
    b) tact
    c) organisational ability
    d) reliability?

4   Practise a number of different interview situations in which *you*
    try to sell yourself to an employer or interviewer. Perform them
    to the rest of the group and comment constructively on any
    relevant points.

22

A

1 **Personnel officer:** Well now perhaps you could tell me what first attracted you to this job.

Interviewee: Er, the money.

2 **Personnel officer:** I see. Now let me ask you about yourself. Do you see yourself as having management potential?

Interviewee: Oh, definitely.

3 **Personnel officer:** Good. That's what we're looking for. Tell me, what sort of person, in your opinion, makes a good manager?

Interviewee: I'm not sure.

4 **Personnel officer:** Let me put it another way: what would you do about an employee who consistently turned up late?

Interviewee: Sack them.

Personnel officer: Just like that?

Interviewee: Well I suppose I might give them a warning first, but you've got to be tough with them. Start as you mean to carry on, that's what I always say.

5 **Personnel officer:** Quite. Now tell me, are you good at dealing with members of the public?

Interviewee: Naturally.

Personnel officer: Well I can see you're confident. But let me put a little problem to you: what would you do if you were faced with a very angry customer demanding a refund?

Interviewee: Well I can be angry too. Nobody puts one past me, I can tell you.

6 **Personnel officer:** Right. Well, last question: we like our staff to look smart; have you seen our uniform?

Interviewee: Yeah.

Personnel officer: And you'd be happy to wear it?

Interviewee: Well I wouldn't exactly say happy, but I can live with it, know what I mean?

B

1 **Personnel officer:** Good afternoon. I'd like you to begin by telling me what first attracted you to this job.

Interviewee: Well I've worked in a big store before, as it says on my application form, and I enjoyed it thoroughly.

2 **Personnel officer:** I see. And do you see yourself as having management potential?

Interviewee: Well I'd like to think so. Of course that's for you to assess. But I think I get on well with people and management is about getting the best out of people, isn't it?

3 **Personnel officer:** Yes that's part of it. It's also about dealing with problems. For example, what would you do about an employee who consistently turned up late?

Interviewee: First I'd consult the store's code of practice in these matters which I presume would suggest the employee be given a verbal warning followed by a written one if the problem continued.

4 **Personnel officer:** And if that had no effect?

Interviewee: Well then I would have no alternative but to terminate that person's contract.

5 **Personnel officer:** And what about an angry customer seeking a refund?

Interviewee: Well that would depend on whether the cause for complaint was genuine, the goods really bought in this shop, and the store's policy in these matters.

6 **Personnel officer:** Okay. Well, just one more question: how do you feel about wearing our uniform?

Interviewee: Fine. I think it lets the customer know who I am as well as protecting my own clothes.

Personnel officer: Thank you very much then.

Talking your way out of...

S/he can talk the hind-legs off a donkey.
Traditional

Persuading

1 **In pairs,** try and persuade your partner:
   a) **who is pretending to be your mother** to let you stay the night at a friend's party
   b) **who is a friend** to cover up for something serious that you have done wrong
   c) **who is a grandparent** to give you some money to buy something you really want
   d) **who is leaving school** to go for a job traditionally associated with the opposite gender.

Complaining

2 **In pairs,** explore some different ways of complaining to a neighbour about the old, rusty car they've had rotting in their front garden for six months.

3 Make a list of all the situations you have to complain about in your normal everyday life. Invent a typical scene in which you are successful!

Excusing

4   Make a list of five realistic excuses for not doing homework.

5   Make up five ingenious excuses for not doing homework.

6   **In pairs,** excuse yourself from a class
    a) to go to an appointment
    b) because you've been sent for but don't want the teacher to
       know
    c) for a personal reason
    d) for no good reason other than you want to 'try it on'.

7   **In pairs,** excuse yourself from a conversation with a friend
    without being rude
    a) because you're late
    b) because you can't stand the person you're with
    c) because you've just remembered something.

Apologising

Some people seem to spend their lives apologising

8   What do you think makes people apologise
    a) for what they are wearing
    b) for the state of their home
    c) for not being good enough at something?

9   Make appropriate apologies for these situations.

You had me fooled

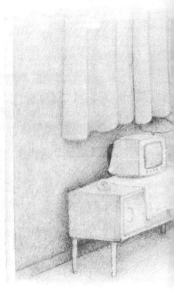

Revenge is a kind of wild justice, which the more man's nature runs to, the more ought law to weed it out.

Francis Bacon

Mr Rudge, an elderly teacher, comes home late one evening. He steps into his living room and turns on the light. He is startled by the scene that meets his eyes.

The man in the chair smiles. 'Remember me?' At first Mr Rudge doesn't but then he says, 'Good Lord! It's Raven.' 'Mr Raven, to you,' the young man says. He tells Rudge that when he was one of Rudge's pupils Rudge picked on him, made a fool out of him, made him feel a failure, made the rest of the class laugh at him. He describes how he grew to hate Rudge and how he grew determined that he would not be a failure. Instead he became a success and he has returned to kill Rudge.

Rudge looks around, horrified. He recognises the chauffeur. He was also a pupil. His name is Dawson. Rudge appeals to him. He says that Dawson was the cleverest boy in the class. How can he now stand there and take orders from Raven?

Dawson is unmoved. Money, he tells Rudge, is the most important thing in life. Mr Raven has lots of money but what does he, Rudge, have? Dawson points round the room at the shabby furniture, the pathetic ornaments, at Rudge himself in his shabby sports-jacket and baggy trousers. If he'd listened to Rudge, he says, he would probably have ended up like him. Instead he'd woken up in time. Now he was only prepared to listen to one kind of talk: money-talk.

Desperately Rudge turns to the two men with the guns. He recognises them, too. They are Smith and Bennet. He begs them not to kill him. Smith looks at him with contempt. What has Rudge ever done for him, he asks. 'At least I didn't pick on you,' Rudge says. 'No,' replies Smith, 'you completely ignored me. You were only interested in clever people like Dawson, or in those you bullied like Mr Raven.' Bennet agrees. 'Just tell me one thing you ever did for us,' he asks, 'just one thing?' Rudge can't think of anything. 'We might as well have been invisible,' Bennet says, 'for all you cared.'

Rudge looks from one to the other. He sees no mercy in their faces. Raven chuckles. 'You see,' he says, 'we all agree. There is only one person in the room who disagrees and that's you, Rudge. Well we can't have that, can we?' He turns to Smith and Bennett. 'Kill him,' he says.

'No, wait,' says Rudge. Then he clutches his throat. He is having a heart-attack. Raven's manner changes. He looks concerned. 'What's the matter with him?' he says. 'Quick, loosen his collar, stretch him out on the sofa, call an ambulance,' he orders in a panic. The others rush about doing all these things. Raven bends over Rudge saying, 'Sir, it was a joke. It was all a joke, sir. Don't die, please don't die.' But it is too late.

1 Talk about the kind of teacher you think Mr Rudge was.

2 Describe his four ex-pupils, Raven, Dawson, Smith and Bennet. Give them first names. Decide on their ages. Agree a role for each one. Decide how they got on at school, what they did when they left, what they are doing now.

3 **In groups of four,** imagine you are each one of the characters. Have the conversation that you might have had when one of you first had the idea of humiliating Mr Rudge. Let all your motives for taking the action emerge clearly.

4 'You were only interested in clever people like Dawson, or in those you bullied like Mr Raven.'
Do you ever feel ignored in class? One psychologist has said that students who lean forward eagerly get most attention from their teachers. Discuss any different ways of gaining attention you have tried or experienced. Try and offer explanations for any generalisations you produce.

5 Imagine that an ambulance has now arrived. Explain to the ambulance driver what has happened.

6 **In a group,** make up and record a scene in which you take a *subtle* revenge on someone who has treated you badly.

Feedback

Far out in the uncharted backwaters of the unfashionable end of the Western Spiral arm of the Galaxy lies a small, unregarded yellow sun.

Orbiting this at a distance of roughly ninety-eight million miles is an utterly insignificant little blue green planet whose ape-descended life forms are so amazingly primitive that they still think digital watches are a pretty neat idea.

The planet has a problem, which was this: most of the people living on it were unhappy for pretty much of the time. Many solutions were suggested for this problem, but most of these were largely concerned with the movements of small green pieces of paper, which is odd because on the whole it wasn't the small green pieces of paper that were unhappy.

From *The Hitch-Hiker's Guide to the Galaxy* by Douglas Adams

1 You arrived on the planet Earth exactly one year ago. You were planted in Britain, given false identities and told to observe as much Earth behaviour as possible. This is your first meeting since arrival.
Begin by describing the role you have adopted in Earth society and what difficulties you have found in playing it.

2 You have each specialised in observing different aspects of human behaviour. They are:
   a) Law, crime and punishment
   b) Education
   c) Money matters
   d) Families
   e) Leisure

Give a report back to the group on what you have discovered about each of these.

3 Do the same for another part of the Earth (not Britain).

4 Are there any aspects of Earth behaviour that you find it difficult to understand?

5 Decide on a fresh list of topics you will observe for the next month.

6 Your Planetary Council wish to make contact with Earth. What advice can you give them? Decide what are the three most important things to remember when dealing with Earth people.

7 Draft a First Message to be beamed down onto all Earth television sets. It should not be too long; it should be friendly but not frightening, powerful but not threatening.

8 What things do you recommend your own society to copy from Earth society?

9 You must make a group decision on whether or not this is the time for making contact.

UNIT 3 GIVING OPINIONS

Starters

Talking about yourself

1 Use this questionnaire to give you ideas for a short talk about yourself.

   a) How do you spend your Saturdays?
   b) What kind of people are you friendly with? Older? Younger? With same interests?
   c) What makes you attracted to someone?
   d) What is your favourite music?
   e) What do you spend most of your free time doing?
   f) What do you like reading?
   g) What do you enjoy most at school? Least?
   h) Describe your family and the area in which you live.
   i) What annoys you most in your life and why?
   j) What would you like to change about yourself if you could?

Example ... 'Well ... I'm Janice and out of school I'm a completely different person. On Saturdays, for example, I work in a vet's surgery...'

Just thirty seconds

Have you ever ... been frightened, been dishonest, cheated someone?

1 For half a minute talk about an experience that has been important for you in your life so far. Pick one of these topics or choose one that means something to you:

   a time you were unfairly treated
   your experience of school
   the most successful thing you've ever done
   a favourite pop group
   something few people know about you
   what you would change if you were
       a) the prime minister
       b) the headteacher of your school.

Description game

Stage 1 **In groups**, write down an untypical but true description of yourself on a piece of paper. Don't include your name. Collect all these pieces of paper in. One person read them all out. Guess which is which.

Stage 2 **In groups**, take it in turns to describe someone known to you all. (S/he could be a well known personality, friend, etc.) See how long you can keep the group guessing the identity of your mystery person, while at the same time saying things about them which are true.

Stage 3 Do the same using characters from fiction, TV or films.

Stage 4 Do the same for mystery objects.

What do you think?

1   Read this extract from a photostory taken from *Blue Jeans*.
    What do you think has happened before it?

2   Talk about a possible continuation for the story.

3   Writers for teenage magazines are often given hints on how to
    write the 'true stories' that readers apparently want to read.
    Talk about the following advice, given by *Patches* magazine.

Language

This should be simple and up-to-date. Avoid the melodramatic, romantic-fiction set phrases which are alien to most adolescents.

Dictionary of phrases to avoid:

> 'I adore you,' he breathed.
> His strong brown arms enfolded me.
> He behaved like a gentleman.
> My heart leapt.
> With one long, loving, lingering look, we parted.

4 Try to concoct your own magazine story.

A programmed discussion

This discussion exercise has been organised in the form of a computer programme.

10   Break up into groups of five. Then go to 20.

20   Select a group representative to make notes. Then go to 30.

30   One member of the group, not the group representative, reads aloud the following story to the other members of the group. Then go to 40.

Story

Someone saw Nasrudin searching for something on the ground.
'What have you lost, Nasrudin?' he asked.
'My key,' Nasrudin replied.
So both the men went down on their knees and looked for it.
After a time the other man asked: 'Where exactly did you lose it?'
'In my own house.'
'Then why are you looking out here?'
'There is more light here than inside my house.'

---

40   This story has a hidden meaning. Each member of the group must answer the following question, separately. The majority answer will be accepted as the group's answer.

Is the hidden meaning to do with
a) the key   **b)** the light?
If you choose **a)** then go to 50. If you choose **b)** then go to 70.

50   **What could the key represent? Consider the following questions:**
   a) When are people ceremonially presented with a key?
   b) What people use keys as part of their job?
   c) Does the word key have any other meanings apart from: metal object for opening lock?

Discuss this. You do not have to reach an opinion. When you are ready go to 60.

60   Perhaps it is the searching for the key that is important. Consider the following questions:
   a) What sort of things do people search for in life?
   b) What do you look for in another person?
   c) What are you going to look for when you leave school? A job? Anything else?

32

Each member of the group should make a list of the three most important aims in her/his life, listed in order. The group representative should write these down. When you have done that go to 80.

70   Consider the idea of light. It's a word that has several meanings. We talk about seeing someone in another light. We talk about throwing some light on a problem and bringing something into the light. Why do you think Nasrudin looks for something where he knows it is not, simply because there is more light there? It is, of course, easier to see in the light, even if there is nothing to see. Each member of the group must honestly tell the group about something which he does, not because it's the right thing to do but simply because it's easier. The group representative should note these down. When you are ready go to 90.

80   When you make any choice, like the choice between a) and b) in question 40, you are prioritising. In other words you are deciding that one item is more important than another – it has a greater priority. This is something we do all the time. We wouldn't be able to take any decisions if we didn't. You have probably already begun to work out the much deeper priorities of your life, your aims. What are your aims in life? Each member of the group make a list of the three most important aims in his/her life, listed in order. The group representative should write these down. When you have done this look at your first priority. You could call this your key-aim, couldn't you? Now consider what the meaning of the key might be in the story. When you are ready go on to 100.

90   Do you think Nasrudin really wants to find the key at all? After all people do sometimes fool others or even themselves about what they are looking for in life. Discuss this. Have you ever noticed anyone doing it? Yourself? Your parents? Your teachers? Your friends? You do not have to reach an opinion. When you are ready to go to 100.

100   What do you think will happen next? Consider the following possibilities:
   a) The other man will explain that Nasrudin is wasting his time and they will both go indoors.
   b) The man will explain but Nasrudin will take no notice.
   c) They will both carry on looking outside.
   d) An alternative suggestion.

   If you chose a), b) or c) then go to 110. If you chose d) then decide what that alternative is, make a note of it, then go to 110.

110   Nasrudin is a fool. Have you ever been in a position where you have made a fool of yourself? Or watched a friend make a fool of him/herself. Tell the group about it. When you are ready go to 130.

120   Plenary session. Compare the conclusions of those who thought the hidden meaning was to do with the key and those who thought it was to do with the light.

Speakers' corner

1 When the Suffragettes began their campaign to get women the vote they met with fierce opposition. One way they found of getting their views heard was to infiltrate another political meeting and suddenly stand up and begin speaking. When one woman was silenced another would immediately carry on with the speech. Read the following fictionalised account of such a meeting and discuss your reactions to it.

She watched Louise get to her feet, unfurling the green, white and purple banner with VOTES FOR WOMEN printed on it. Listen . . . she must listen! The words of the speech she had read a hundred times were rolling from Louise's tongue, her resonant voice filling every corner of the Hall. No reaction; people stunned; even the man on the platform hesitated. A long, long moment.

'Suffragettes!' The cry was picked up in different parts of the Hall, then: 'Shame . . . throw her out!'

Four burly men were making their way down the aisles on either side. The men and women seated beside Louise turned on her, snatching the banner. Officials closed in, pushing along the row, treading on toes. There was no escape, but still she went on speaking:

'. . . as the world looks on. It is the shame of England that half its population should be treated thus, denied the privilege, as are convicts, and . . .' Her part was done. Half dragged, unresisting, the cloak torn from her shoulders, Louise was hurried into the aisle and ejected from the Hall.

But the speech was not over.

'Convicts and lunatics,' boomed a voice with the power of a foghorn. 'Is this the mark of a mature and well-tried civilisation, or will in years to come the finger of derision and scorn be pointed at . . .'

Fury seething and wrestling with her unstable stomach, Emily watched the horsy woman roughly shoved from the body of the Hall. And still the speech was flowing. Another woman banished trailing shreds of tulle and veiling. The fourth was Mary Grant, her deep voice compelling attention, conquering the noise of the angry crowd. Emily would be next.

From *A Question of Courage* by Marjorie Darke

2 Imagine that the government had decided to withdraw the right to vote from everyone who had been unemployed for more than six months. As unemployed persons you wish to protest but all public speeches on the matter have been banned. **In your group**, work out your speech and be prepared to deliver it. Each member may be stopped at the discretion of the class at any point in the speech. Every other member must be ready to carry on immediately.

3 You have decided to make a banner which briefly states your main arguments in slogan form. At the top of the banner you have written: VOTES FOR THE UNEMPLOYED BECAUSE...
In pairs, decide what to write next.

4 If you had to make a speech supporting the government's action, what are the main arguments that you would use? Draw up a list of five reasons why the government has decided on this course of action.

5 The right of free speech has always been regarded as one of Britain's most important possessions. Make a list of all the reasons you can think of in defence of this right.

6 Are there any matters about which you should not be allowed to speak freely? List them, if you think so.

Developing an argument

> Rightly to be great
> Is not to stir without great argument...
>
> *Shakespeare*

1 Animal experiments are necessary and beneficial to society. Do you agree with this statement?

2 Many people would disagree with this view – some violently. Follow the arguments that The Research Defence Society makes on this controversial topic.

For all our sakes science still needs animals

The facts

- Faced with a severe illness or a critically ill relative, most people do not hesitate to have their doctor prescribe an effective medicine which will have been thoroughly tested, using animals.

- Even ardent anti-vivisectionists do not want to see their pets die, if an animal-tested medicine can save their lives, or a vaccine prevent infection.

- Few would refrain from suing a manufacturer whose product disfigured or damaged them.

- At work, trade unionists and safety representatives demand safety data, based on animal studies, on substances they handle.

- 80 per cent of all animal experiments in Britain are for medical, dental or veterinary advancement. The remainder are for the protection of consumers or *workers in industry*.

- In the past 50 years, medical research expenditure has increased, in real terms, 40-fold. In the same period the number of animal experiments had increased only 25-fold.

- There has been a *steady decrease in animal experiments* in the last ten years.

- We eat more than 400 million animals (cattle, pigs and poultry) each year in Britain – about 7 each.

- Over 80% of all experiments involve rats or mice. Dogs account for only 0.25% and cats 0.14% of the total. The RSPCA kills very large numbers of unwanted cats and dogs every year – many times the number used in all UK laboratories.

These are a few examples of the double standards we all apply but prefer to overlook.

However, we must ensure that those animals that *have* to be used are properly safeguarded.

There are alternatives

These are being used whenever they prove scientifically valid and acceptable to the authorities.

But at present, and for a long time to come, there is no alternative to the majority of tests.

Pharmaceutical research

Here are a few examples of diseases which have been virtually eliminated through animal research:

smallpox
tuberculosis.
whooping cough
measles
infection after burns.

Society faces a dilemma. We want better medicines and safer products but some want to deny the scientist the means to achieve these ends. But they cannot have it both ways – or can they?

From *The Research Defence Society*

3   It is sometimes easier to see different techniques being used in an argument when the case being made is a difficult one. Talk about which of these skills you think The Research Defence Society is using:
    a) organising material
    b) selecting material
    c) developing a clear progression of ideas
    d) using a variety of methods of presentation
    e) looking at other points of view
    f) exposing bias or prejudice
    g) using appropriate vocabulary
    h) asking good questions
    i) exploring the implications of an opinion.

4   Which of them are used most effectively in this case? Do you think this is a good argument, whether or not you agree with it? Are other techniques being used here?

Terrorism

1　Brainstorm all the associations that the word 'terrorist' has for you.

2　Read these four accounts of violent incidents in different countries. For each one agree a) where it happened b) what the nature of the violent activity was.

a) It was a Friday night in Birmingham, England, 21 November 1974. The pubs were filling up. Two, in particular, where crowded – the Mulberry Bush and the Tavern of the Town, both in the centre of the city. Suddenly, just after eight o'clock, explosions ripped their way through the buildings. In the horror and confusion, twenty-one people lay dead, one hundred and sixty-two were injured. It was an IRA bomb attack.

b) In March 1968 an American company of soldiers, under Lieutenant William Calley, entered a Vietnamese village called My Lai. They had been brutalized and demoralized by war. Their orders were to 'clean up' the village, though what this should involve was not clear. On Calley's orders, they began to shoot the villagers. Over five hundred civilians died.

c) In May 1972 members of a Japanese group, who had formed links with the Popular Front for the Liberation of Palestine, managed to get into Lod Airport in Israel. They opened fire with machine guns at waiting passengers. Twenty-six were killed and eighty wounded. Most were Puerto Rican pilgrims who had been visiting the Holy Land.

d) Between 1936 and 1939 there was a civil war in Spain. The government was faced with an uprising which was supported by the Fascist governments of Germany and Italy. The people of the Basque region of Spain supported the government. On 26 April 1937 the church bells rang out a warning in Guernica, a small town in the Basque region. Half an hour later German bombers appeared over the undefended town and the bombing began. The centre of the town was left in flames and perhaps a thousand civilians were killed.

From *Terrorism* by Charles Freeman.

3　Would you describe all four as terrorist incidents?
In pairs, list your reasons.

4　**In pairs,** make a list of the differences and the similarities between the incidents.

5　Try to agree on a definition of the word terrorism.

6　Apart from the incidents you have just read about, what other sorts of activities do terrorists engage in? Talk about any examples you know of.

7　What people and things in our society are most at risk from terrorism? Agree a list.

8 Terrorists generally justify their actions on the grounds that they are freedom-fighters trying to gain liberation for their people. Read the following extract from the autobiography of Leila Khaled, a Palestinian terrorist. She describes how she felt while waiting to board an aeroplane she would later hijack. Talk about your reactions to it.

> I noticed an American lady with four young children who seemed very happy and excited about their trip. I then realised with a shock that something dreadful could happen to them if anything went wrong. I love children and I wanted to tell the lady not to travel on this flight. But when I thought of our Palestinian children who had nothing in life, I felt a bit stronger and braver.
>
> From *My People Shall Live* by L. Khaled.

9 Without knowing anything about the conflict in Palestine, what could you have said to Ms Khaled to have persuaded her *not* to hijack the plane?

10 One attempt to counter terrorism was *The Prevention of Terrorism Act*, which came into force in Britain on 29 November 1974. However, in many people's opinions, the act has been unsuccessful. Read the following information about the Act.

> Between 1974 and 1984, 5896 people were arrested under the P.T.A. but fewer than 2.5% were ever charged. Fewer than 50% of those charged received a prison sentence. Of those who did, a number are the subject of controversy due to uncertain evidence. In all, 5749 people were detained for periods ranging from a few hours to seven days and then released without charge.
>
> The Greater London Council conducted a survey of those arrested under the P.T.A. in the London area. All of those arrested were denied access to a solicitor and effectively disappeared because neither family nor friends were informed of their detention. Detainees complained of physical and mental ill-treatment. Some required medical assistance following release. At least one required long-term medical treatment; some lost their employment and found that their families had been subjected to harassment. Children were placed in care, families broken up and at least one suicide occurred.
>
> *GLC Report on the Prevention of Terrorism Act*

11 Talk about what your first reaction would be if you heard that a person in your street had been detained under *The Prevention of Terrorism Act*.

12 Would it make a difference to how you felt if you heard that s/he had been released three days later without being charged with any offence?

13 If that person then lost her/his job when the employer was told, should that person be compensated? Give clear reasons **for** or **against**.

14 If so, how much money would you give to someone who had lost a £10,000 a year job and had two children under five and one dependent adult? Justify your decision.

Nuclear energy

1 Brainstorm all the associations that the phrase 'nuclear energy' has for you.

2 Read these opinions about nuclear energy and nuclear waste.

a) Energy is essential for survival. All methods of producing energy, however, can cause some damage to the environment and to health.

In each case the harm has to be weighed against the benefits that arise from the availability of the energy source. In the case of nuclear power the principal benefit is the large potential contribution to the world's energy resources, releasing fossil fuels for other essential purposes such as transport, industrial process heat, and raw material for chemicals and fertilisers. Furthermore the total impact on the health of workers and the public is no greater and probably less than that of fossil fuels.

UK Atomic Energy Authority

b) Britain has a glut of energy. It's an island with over 300 years' reserves of coal sitting in a sea of oil and gas, with the longest coastline in Europe – good for wind, tidal and wave sources of energy. Most other EEC countries are envious of our huge energy reserves. Nuclear power only supplies about 4% of our total energy needs, and it supplies it in a form – electricity – which is either impractical or too expensive for the vast majority of our energy needs – industrial and domestic heating.

Because of the large generating reserves held in Britain, we could switch off our nine operating nuclear stations tomorrow with little difficulty.

Friends of the Earth

c) The radiation dose from the natural background varies from place to place in the UK by over a factor of two. However, we know from the experience of many generations that this variation is of no significance to health. The maximum extra radiation dose to any member of the public from nuclear electricity generation is less than this natural variation. The risk, therefore, is of no practical concern.

United Kingdom Atomic Energy Authority

d) Mining uranium, the fuel for nuclear power stations, produces huge amounts of solid and liquid waste. For every 1000 tonnes of uranium fuel 100,000 tonnes of radioactive solid waste (known as tailings) and 3,500,000 litres of liquid waste are produced. The radioactivity, carried by wind and water, can contaminate the environment and increase the local rate of cancers. For example, an investigation carried out by the US Government estimated that the rate of lung cancer within 1.5 km of a pile of tailings is likely to increase by 14%.

Friends of the Earth

3   Comment on the contrasting opinions of nuclear power on the previous page.

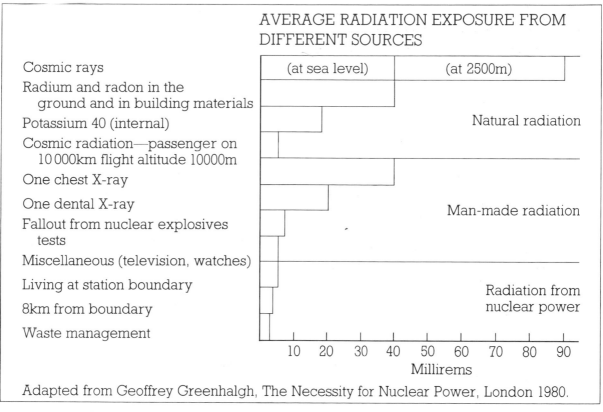

AVERAGE RADIATION EXPOSURE FROM DIFFERENT SOURCES

Cosmic rays

Radium and radon in the ground and in building materials

Potassium 40 (internal)

Cosmic radiation—passenger on 10 000km flight altitude 10000m

One chest X-ray

One dental X-ray

Fallout from nuclear explosives tests

Miscellaneous (television, watches)

Living at station boundary

8km from boundary

Waste management

(at sea level)   (at 2500m)

Natural radiation

Man-made radiation

Radiation from nuclear power

Millirems

Adapted from Geoffrey Greenhalgh, The Necessity for Nuclear Power, London 1980.

International Atomic Energy Agency February, 1981

4   What does this chart tell us? Does it contradict anything you have just read or already knew?

5   Make a list of all the other alternative sources of power that *you* know about.

6   For each one, without going into too much detail, discuss:
    a) its advantages
    b) its disadvantages.

For the following tasks you will need to do further preparation work.

7   How difficult do you think it is to get an unbiased picture of:
    a) the nuclear industry
    b) alternative energy sources
    c) Britain's future energy needs
    d) possible energy-saving strategies?

8   Write to as many different sources as you can to find out about nuclear energy. (See page 95).

9   Assemble as much information on this subject as you can from newspapers and magazines.

10 Using the research you have done into nuclear power, prepare a five minute talk on the subject.

UNIT 4 WRITING TOGETHER

Starters

Not now Bernard

This is a children's story by David McKee. The first (A) and the last (Q) lines are in the right order. Agree a sensible order for the rest of it.

A   'Hello, Dad,' said Bernard. 'Not now Bernard,' said his father.

B   The monster ate Bernard up, every bit. Then the monster went inside.

C   'Your dinner's ready,' said Bernard's mother.

D   Then it read one of Bernard's comics. And broke one of his toys.

E   The monster went upstairs.

F   'Go to bed. I've taken up your milk,' called Bernard's mother.

G   'Hello Mum,' said Bernard. 'Not now, Bernard,' said his mother.

H   'There's a monster in the garden and it's going to eat me,' said Bernard.

I   The monster ate the dinner. Then it watched television.

J   She put the dinner in front of the television.

K   The monster bit Bernard's father. 'Not now, Bernard,' said Bernard's father.

L   'Not now, Bernard, said his mother.

M   Bernard went into the garden.

N   'Not now, Bernard,' said Bernard's mother.

O   'ROAR,' went the monster behind Bernard's mother.

P   'Hello monster,' he said to the monster.

Q   'But I'm a monster,' said the monster. 'Not now, Bernard,' said Bernard's mother.

[Answers on page 90]

Story-games

In groups of three, complete these stories by adding your own bit everywhere you see three dots, like this . . .

At Janie's wedding

1st Person: Haven't I seen you before somewhere?

2nd Person: I don't think so.

1st Person: Yes I have. It was at Janie's wedding. You should remember; you were . . .

3rd Person: Well fancy meeting you two here. The last time I saw you, you were making complete fools of yourselves. You were . . .

2nd Person: You talk about us making fools of ourselves. At least we didn't . . .

In the bunker

1st Person: Cheer up you say! Listen I've been in this shelter for weeks, the world's probably been blown up, we've run out of food and you say I should cheer up. Just give me one good reason why I should.

2nd Person: All right then I will . . .

3rd Person: You two have got a nerve, standing there talking as if I don't exist. I know why you've been ignoring me. It's because . . .

Missing words

Ten words have been missed out in this poem. Decide on the words you think would be most suitable.

Disruptive Minority

Rude words on the blackboard,
Crushed chalk on the floor,
Books, bunged out the window,
Run out, slam the door.

_____ depression,
Me and my class.
Football in the playground
Connects with school _____.

_____ in the toilet
And nudie books too.
When I leave this _____
Then what will I do?

I'm nothing _____,
The _____ taught me that.
I haven't got _____
And my _____ are flat.

Can't hit back at the system
It's _____, has no features,
So while I'm at school
I'll take it out on the _____.

Alan Gilbey

[The original words are on page 90.]

Dateline

In groups, try and decide when each of these extracts was written. Match them to these date periods. Give your reasons fully.

a) 1600–1650
b) 1750–1850
c) 1900–1920
d) 1930–1950
e) 1960–1980

1   This is the story of Noah. Noah was a righteous man, the one blameless man of his time; he walked with God. He had three sons, Shem, Ham and Japheth. Now God saw that the whole world was corrupt and full of violence.

2   Pack-up your troubles in your old kit bag
And smile, smile, smile,
While you've a lucifer to light your fag,
Smile boy that's the style.

3   These are the generations of Noah: Noah was a just man and perfect in his generations, and Noah walked with God. And Noah begat three sons, Shem, Ham and Japheth. The earth also was corrupt before God, and the earth was filled with violence.

4   It is a truth universally acknowledged that a single man in possession of a good fortune must be in want of a wife.

5   What has Uncle Quentin done now? Julian winked at Dick, and kicked George under the table. Would Uncle Quentin explode into a temper, as he sometimes did?

[Answers on page 90.]

Story-shaping

The first stories were not made up by one person but by lots of people over a period of time, adding and altering bits. We call these stories myths or legends.

The question is – do people shape stories or do stories shape people?

1 Consider the following story:

THESEUS AND THE LABYRINTH

The town of Athens had been conquered by the army of Crete. When the Athenians asked King Minos of Crete what he would accept in return for not destroying their town utterly, he said that every year the people of Athens must send to Crete seven young men and seven young women. These he would give as food to that terrible monster the Minotaur. The Minotaur was half man and half bull and it lived in a maze of passages called The Labyrinth.

The sacrifice went on year after year until one day Theseus, the king's own son, decided to go as one of the young men. The king could not persuade him otherwise.

Theseus was a great warrior and he was determined to kill the Minotaur. He told his father that he would change the black sails that the ship bore to white if he killed the beast.

When the party, led by Theseus, arrived, the king of Crete laughed to see Theseus. But his daughter, Ariadne, did not laugh. She pitied the young people and she fell in love with Theseus. She decided to help him. Theseus' main problem was that even if he slew the monster, he would never find his way back out of the Labyrinth. But Ariadne gave him a ball of thread which he fastened to the entrance gate. He kept hold of the thread and wandered through the maze. At last he found the creature and, after a terrible struggle, killed it. He found his way back to the gate again by winding up the thread. Then, with Adriadne's help, the young people escaped that night. Theseus took Ariadne to be his bride.

However one thing was forgotten. In their excitement, they did not remember to change the sails on the boat. When they got near Athens the old king saw the black sails and guessed that his son was dead. Before the boat, with its happy party, returned to shore, the old king had died of grief.

---

2 Talk about these statements:
   a) The title 'Theseus and the Labyrinth' is sexist. It might just as well be called 'Ariadne and the Labyrinth'.
   b) Ariadne would never have left Crete on her own.
   c) Ariadne may have had other reasons for leaving Crete than falling in love.
   d) A woman as clever as Ariadne would hardly be 'taken' back by Theseus to be his bride.
   e) Theseus does not seem to have been very clever.
   f) Women are likely to fall in love with strong men.

3 Compare the answers given by girls to those given by boys.

4   Change the story by telling it from Ariadne's point of view. Use this outline:

    a) What Ariadne's life was like before Theseus' arrival
    b) Theseus' arrival and her decision to help him
    c) How the monster was slain
    d) The escape
    e) What happened after

5   Make up two different versions of what happened when they returned to Athens: a happy one and an unhappy one.

6   Read this story of Cinderella retold by Roald Dahl.
(The Ugly Sisters have both pretended that the glass slipper fits them. Rather than marry either of them, the Prince has chopped off their heads.)

CINDERELLA

Poor Cindy's heart was torn to shreds.
My Prince! she thought. He chops off *heads*!
How could I marry anyone
Who does that sort of thing for fun?
The Prince cried, 'Who's this dirty slut?
'Off with her nut! Off with her nut!'
Just then all in a blaze of light,
The Magic Fairy hove in sight,
Her magic wand went swoosh and swish!
'Cindy!' she cried, 'come make a wish!'
'Wish anything and have no doubt
'That I will make it come about!'
Cindy answered, 'Oh kind Fairy,
'This time I shall be more wary.
'No more Princes, no more money.
'I have had my taste of honey.
'I'm wishing for a decent man.
'They're hard to find. D'you think you can?'
Within a minute, Cinderella
Was married to a lovely feller,
A simple jam-maker by trade,
Who sold good home-made marmalade.
Their house was filled with smiles and laughter
And they were happy ever after.

From *Revolting Rhymes* by Roald Dahl

7   Talk about these statements:

    a) Nobody ever lives happily ever after.
    b) Stories like Cinderella teach children ideas about life that do not turn out to be true.
    c) It's only a fairy story.
    d) Every girl is looking for Mr Right.
    e) Every girl wants to be swept off her feet.

8   Make up a new story in which Cinderella goes from rags to riches, though not by marrying a Prince.

Creating a radio play

1 You are going to make a radio play about someone called Beta Orvet who was born in a country called Icarus. Read the details of Orvet's life printed below.

Background

Icarus is a country where there is a great deal of social injustice. The gulf between rich and poor is great. Criticism of society is something only carried on in whispers in Icarus.

Beta Orvet is a scientist who has three times won the International Babel Prize for work on bio-engineering.

Sequence of events

a) Orvet sent by post a letter criticising society to prominent politicians, professors, civil-servants, journalists, television and radio controllers and even people apparently chosen at random from a telephone book.

b) Orvet was summoned by the Chancellor of the University which sponsored the research project Orvet led. The Chancellor said that everyone at the University was very sorry. Then Orvet was led away by Intelligence Officers.

c) Orvet was imprisoned and was visited by another scientist who said the arrest and imprisonment had caused an international sensation.

e) Orvet was made welcome in Mersia, and made Head of another research project at another university.

g) Orvet was summoned by the Chancellor of the University and taken away again, this time to the frontier with Icarus.

d) Orvet was summoned by the Prison Governor who said contemptuously that friends in Mersia would now look after Orvet. Orvet was mystified but no explanation was given. Again Orvet was led away, taken to the frontier and handed over to Mersian Intelligence Officers.

f) It did not take Orvet long to see that Mersia was just as corrupt and repressive as Icarus. On realising this, Orvet wrote an identical letter to professors, politicians, civil-servants and others, criticising Mersian society.

h) At the frontier there was a confused incident. Unknown persons came driving furiously towards the border from both directions. Shots were fired by guards on either side. Orvet was killed. Each side blamed the other for setting the incident up.

2 Make a list of the characters you will need. You may need more than those mentioned in the account above, in order to make it easier to tell the story.

3 Make a list of the number of scenes you will need. You may decide to have some of the action told, either by a narrator or by one character telling another.

4 Practise each scene before you decide on a final version.

5 Record your play on tape using the script you have agreed upon. Include sound effects, if possible.

The Charlotte Dymond case

The Ballad of Charlotte Dymond

It was a Sunday evening
And in the April rain
That Charlotte went from our house
And never came home again.

Her shawl of diamond redcloth
She wore a yellow gown,
She carried the green gauze handkerchief
She bought in Bodmin town.

About her throat her necklace
And in her purse her pay:
The four silver shillings
She had at Lady Day.

In her purse four shillings
And in her purse her pride.
As she walked out one evening
Her lover at her side.

Out beyond the marshes
Where the cattle stand,
With her crippled lover
Limping at her hand.

Charlotte walked with Matthew
Through the Sunday mist,
Never saw the razor
Waiting at his wrist.

Charlotte she was gentle
But they found her in the flood
Her Sunday beads among the reeds
Beaming with her blood.

Matthew, where is Charlotte,
And wherefore has she flown?
For you walked out together
And now are come alone.

Why do you not answer,
Stand silent as a tree,
Your Sunday worsted stockings
All muddied to the knee?

Why do you mend your breast-pleat
With a rusty needle's thread
And fall with fears and silent tears
Upon your single bed?

Why do you sit so sadly
Your face the colour of clay
And with a green gauze handkerchief
Wipe the sour sweat away?

Has she gone to Blisland
To seek an easier place?
And is that why your eye won't dry
And blinds your bleaching face?

'Take me home!' cried Charlotte,
'I lie here in the pit!
A red rock rests upon my breasts
And my naked neck is split!'

Her skin was soft as sable,
Her eyes were wide as day,
Her hair was blacker than the bog
That licked her life away.

Her cheeks were made of honey.
Her throat was made of flame
Where all around the razor
Had written its red name.

As Matthew turned at Plymouth
About the tilting Hoe,
The cold and cunning Constable
Up to him did go.

'I've come to take you, Matthew,
Unto the Magistrate's door.
Come quiet now, you pretty poor boy,
And you must know what for.'

'She is as pure,' cried Matthew,
'As is the early dew,
Her only stain it is the pain
That round her neck I drew!'

'She is as guiltless as the day
She sprang forth from her mother.
The only sin upon her skin
Is that she loved another.'

They took him off to Bodmin,
They pulled the prison bell,
They sent him smartly up to Heaven
And dropped him down to Hell.

All through the granite kingdom
And on its travelling airs
Ask which of these two lovers
The most deserves your prayers.

And your steel heart search, Stranger
That you may pause and pray
For lovers who come not to bed
Upon their wedding day.

But lie upon the moorland
Where stands the sacred snow
Above the breathing river,
And the salt sea-winds go.

Charles Causley

1 When do you think this poem was set? What evidence is there in the poem for your answer?

2 Why do you think Matthew and Charlotte were described as lovers? Does the fact that Matthew was crippled affect your answer? Why?

3 Make a list of all the people mentioned in the poem.

4 Make a list of six people who *might* have been important in this story but who are not included in the poem. Justify your selection.

Example:

Lady Barrington (Charlotte's employer who had known her for three years and had strong views about her!)

5 Imagine that Charlotte has **just** been killed. You are a News TV team. You have been sent by your editor to Bodmin to investigate the crime for your Evening News Programme. You are aiming to produce a series of interviews probing into the background to the case. One of you will act as a link person giving your group's interpretation of the events.

   a) Decide on six characters to interview who might be able to reveal something about Charlotte and Matthew that isn't already known.
   b) Write out your interview as a script.
   c) Present your programme.

News and views

1   Read these three accounts of a decision taken by the Mulworth Borough Council.

COUNCIL PROVIDES FREE CREMATION

Mulworth Council announced their decision to provide a free cremation for deceased residents. Ratepayers have complained that, at a price of nearly £400 per head, the cost will be enormous.

NOW IT'S DEATH ON THE DOLE

High-spending Mulworth has done it again!

Not satisfied with spending years subsidising life on the dole for its 35% unemployed workforce, the council – second in the Government's table for spendthrift councils – now wants to pay for their deaths as well.

The Council is providing a £400 funeral service and cremation – half the going rate – for residents in the Borough. The package is free, of course, to Mulworth's 11,000 unemployed.

Will we see Mulworth become the cheapest place to die? What a recommendation.

BURY THOSE FUNERAL COSTS

It's the end of the line for the grief-merchants who make money out of other people's misery. The Council have drawn up an agreement with the Noriss and National Insurance Company to make available to residents with deceased relatives a dignified service and cremation. The Council has further agreed to meet the entire cost itself in the case of residents in receipt of state-benefit.

Council Leader, Sid Bantry, said: 'We believe that those who have given their years to the Borough should be guaranteed a respectful farewell when they take their leave of it.'

2　For each of these newspaper items decide:

    a) what attitude the paper takes to the Council's decision
    b) which of the three is the most neutral.

3　Decide on one word which sums up the style of each item.

4　For each of the following 'neutral' articles, write two contrasting versions in the style of, for example, *The Sun* or *The Mirror* or *The Morning Star* or any other newspaper you know. For each one make up an eye-catching headline.

Women's Hospital To Close

The Western Regional Health Authority today announced plans for the closure of the Lady Tomkins Women's Hospital. The hospital, founded in 1867, is the only hospital in the area specializing in treating women. A spokesperson for the health authority said that financial reasons had dictated the decision.

Parents To Be Charged For School Books

In future parents of pupils at schools in the North-East will be expected to meet the cost of school textbooks, it was decided today. By this measure the government hopes to save £3 million which they say will be used to make badly-needed structural repairs to schools in the area.

Councillors Probe Behind Iron Curtain

Three Labour councillors set off today for a two-week visit to Moscow. The trip, paid for by the Soviet Communist Party, is at the invitation of the Soviet Premier, Mr Gorbachov.

5　Read a variety of newspapers printed on the same day. Find a story which appears in more than one paper. Talk about any differences.

    Look in particular for:
      the choice of vocabulary
      the difficulty of the article
      the use of headlines
      the use of quotations
      the use of pictures
      the attitudes expressed

School with a view

1 **In groups,** compare these two prospectuses of two different imaginary schools. Discuss what you learn about each school.

Front cover

THE DOVER SCHOOL

HEADMISTRESS

Miss P. R. Chalker M.A.

Inside front cover

The aims of the school

1. To promote the highest possible standards of academic achievement.
2. To equip all pupils for a successful life ahead.
3. To help pupils to take responsibility and contribute to the life of the community.
4. ...

Newbridge Health Warning: Learning can seriously stimulate and interest you here.

We hope that all students and their parents will read this carefully: it has been written by staff *and* students.

There is only one rule at Newbridge: We show respect to all people and to their property.

2   What kind of school is your own? Is it large, small, comprehensive, independent, single-sex, co-educational?

3   Comment on Dover School's aims. Are they like any that you have in your own school? Agree a list of the five aims that you think best sum up what your school is trying to do.

4   Brainstorm all the ingredients that you would include if you were designing a prospectus for a school.

Examples
school hours/timetable
map
clubs
who's who
new subjects, etc.

5   Decide on a suitable order for these to appear in. (This can eventually form the basis for a Contents Page.)

6   Decide on a style for your prospectus,
e.g. 'pupils' or 'students' or 'you'
e.g. should it have illustrations, colour etc?

7   Decide on different responsibilities within your group. Make a list of what each individual member is going to contribute or write.

8   Make up a prospectus for your school **or** make up an 'alternative' and unofficial booklet in which you are totally open and honest about everything that really goes on.

Remember
Think who is going to read it.
Think about what would be most useful for your readers to know.
Try and make your prospectus as original as possible.

UNIT 5 INVESTIGATING THE MEDIA

Starters

Examining your own image

> The apparel oft proclaims the man.
> *Shakespeare*, sixteenth century

> She wears her clothes, as if they were thrown on her with a pitchfork.
> *Swift*, eighteenth century

In the twentieth century, television and film have made everyone even more conscious of image.

1 What images do these pictures present? Do the people shown care about how they look? Who or what are they appealing to? Does 'class' come into it? Style? Age? Protest?

2 Talk about the different images presented by this same student.

Images in advertising

1 Look at the two advertisements on the right: one is for health food, the other for fitted kitchens.

Talk about:
a) the way women are portrayed in them
b) the language used
c) how effective you think they are as advertisements.

Thinking before speaking

'That corner's an accident black-spot!'

'The history of the world is dominated by a few important statesmen.'

1 Look at these two sentences and talk about any words which might be considered offensive or irritating by some people.

2 Explore the meanings behind these words: StatesMEN and BLACK-spot.

3 What are the implications of these words?

Headmaster	coloured
housewife	crippled
hero	spastic
blacken	white-wash

4 Make a list of as many words as possible which imply attitudes.

IS THIS YOUR HUSBAND'S IDEA OF A BALANCED DIET?

A quick bite and a pint of wallop?

Or perhaps a take-away burger and chips, instant soups, a packet of crisps or just a bar of chocolate?

Fortunately there's another way to safeguard your vitamin and mineral levels.

The Healthcrafts range of food supplements.

Your first visit to a Poggenpohl studio can be a rather unusual experience.

Unlike the average kitchen salesman, a Poggenpohl specialist is a unique combination of designer and retailer.

Why is this man so interested in your wife?

Spotting bias

A statesman is an easy man
He tells his lies by rote.
A journalist makes up his lies
And takes you by the throat   *W. B. Yeats*

1 Read the following extract from a letter published by *The Daily Telegraph* in 1985:

> I have recently returned from a two-month tour of South Africa. In one town, I was appalled but not surprised to see a television crew encouraging schoolchildren to run towards them, as if rioting. When they had complied, they were told to go back and do it again, and wave their fists and try to look more ferocious.
>
> *Mr Evans, Torpoint, Devon*

2 A South African minister said that this was evidence that foreign TV crews paid youths to stage riots. Reporters were banned from many areas of South Africa. How convincing do you find this evidence?

3 Later, another newspaper investigated the letter. They discovered the following facts:

   a) The only Torpoint in England is in Cornwall, not Devon.
   b) The people living at the address given were a Mr & Mrs Crocker who knew nothing about the letter.
   c) There were two Evanses living in Torpoint. Neither had written the letter.

   Who do **you** think wrote the letter, and why?

4 *The Daily Telegraph* should obviously have checked before publishing that letter. Sometimes, though, it isn't as simple as getting the facts wrong. Read the report at the top of the next page of a school in Tottenham, North London. The report appeared not long after Tottenham had been the site of severe rioting in which a policeman was stabbed to death.

SCHOOL FOR OLD-FASHIONED VALUES

Strains of hymns ancient and modern drift out into the corridor outside the headmaster's study. A group of noisy little girls larking about in an unattended classroom are put firmly in their place by a woman teacher. Staff and pupils pause to smile and nod at visitors waiting at the inquiry desk.

But this remarkable monument to traditional academic values is no cloistered educational palace. It lies in the heart of Tottenham – the London borough torn apart by October's terrible riots. All but a handful of the 310 pupils aged 9 to 18 are of West Indian origin. Unlike many of the nearby comprehensives, it has little truck with the trendy ideas many now believe are behind the surge in juvenile crime and civil disorder.

The fee-paying John Loughborough school, owned and run by the Seventh Day Adventists ... gears its teaching towards the society in which its pupils will have to make a living – not their ethnic background as advocated by the Inner London Education Authority. Here's the headmaster on the curriculum: 'We do teach the history of the Caribbean but at the end of the day they won't be sitting their exams in the Caribbean.'

Daily Express 5.12.84

5 What does the middle paragraph tell you about the writer's views on education?

6 Sometimes newspapers make no attempt to disguise their political sympathies. Read this extract from an article also published in the Daily Express:

> LOONY LEFT BANS A CHRISTMAS CRIB
> A loony left council has refused permission for the Nativity Scene to be enacted on land that it owns. They fear it could cause offence to other religious groups.

7 What do you think of the Council's decision?

8 What do you think of the description, 'loony left'?

9 Compare the two photographs reproduced below. Both are of the South African woman, Winnie Mandela. Do they give different impressions?

a)

b)

10 What effect do the words 'black power' have in the caption below photograph **a**)? Would it make a difference if they were replaced by the word 'victory'?

11 What captions would you use for these two pictures?

Playgroup politics

1 The pictures printed below are from a child's picture book. The story begins with a ring at the doorbell. Now read on . . .

Sophie's Mummy said,
"I wonder who that can be.

It can't be the milkman because he came this morning.

And it can't be the boy from the grocer because this isn't the day he comes.

And it can't be Daddy because he's got his key.

We'd better open the door and see."

2 Study the pictures carefully and then make a chart like the one printed below.

Character	Gender	Clothing	Attitude	Objects
Mummy	Female			
Grocer's boy	Male			
Milkman	Male			
Daddy	Male			

Under the heading *Clothing* write either outdoor or indoor.
Under the heading *Attitude* write either purposeful or uncertain.

Under the heading *Objects* write down any objects that appear in the pictures, associated with each character.

3 What does this chart tell us about the hidden message the pictures convey?

4 The visitor was a tiger who consumed all the food and drink in the house. Study the following pictures carefully and decide what hidden messages they convey. For example, is it significant that in the second picture it is Daddy who is buttoning up the girl's coat? Make a list of ways in which these messages are conveyed.

Sophie's Mummy said, "I don't know what to do. I've got nothing for Daddy's supper, the tiger has eaten it all."

And Sophie's Daddy said, "I know what we'll do. I've got a very good idea. We'll put on our coats and go to a café."

5 What effect do you think pictures like these have on young children?

6 Design a warning, like the Government Health Warning which appears on cigarette packets, advising parents of the effects of books like these upon their children.

7 Look at the next set of pictures. They are quite open about their message. Do you think this sort of thing should or should not appear in books for young children?

Some people have nowhere to live

even though many houses remain empty.

Television advertisements

 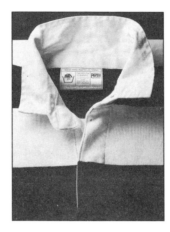 

1 Do you recognise these famous advertisements? Talk about five TV advertisements that you know. Say why you think they're effective.

2 Talk about any of this information relating to TV advertising that you consider interesting.

   a) The Broadcasting Act (1981) gives the Independent Broadcasting Authority (IBA) the power and duty to exclude misleading advertisements.

   b) The IBA Code of Advertising Standards and Practice regulates what advertisements should be shown.

   c) Approximately 18% of scripts are returned to advertisers to be amended.

   d) If you have a complaint you can write to The Advertising Control Division, IBA, 70 Brompton Road, LONDON.

   e) TV advertising is limited to 6 minutes an hour averaged out over the day's programmes. Radio normally has a maximum of 9 minutes.

6 mins an hour   9 mins an hour

3   Consider what the IBA Code says about alcohol, children, health and exaggeration.

Alcoholic drink

'... no-one associated with drinking in an advertisement should seem to be younger than 25 ... no liquor advertisement may feature any personality whose example young people are likely to follow...'

Children

'Advertisements must not directly urge children to purchase or to ask their parents or others to make enquiries or purchases.'

Health

'Advertisements for confectionery or snack foods shall not suggest that such products may be substituted for proper meals.'

Exaggeration

'No advertisement shall make exaggerated claims.'

For each of these statements, think of any advertisements you know which come closest to disobeying them.
Can you think of any that actually seem not to comply with them?

4   What products do you think cannot be advertised on television?

[Answers on page 90]

5   Despite these safeguards there are people who feel that television advertising still gives an unrealistic and unfair view of the world, for example, of women, family life, ethnic minorities. Discuss any advertisements you know which fall into these categories and say why.

6   There are strong arguments for and against television advertising. Discuss this and organise three powerful arguments **for** or **against** it.

7   Make up your own advertisement using video (if you can) or alternatively radio (i.e. tape).
Decide what you're going to advertise, e.g. your school, a product, a campaign.

Write the accompanying script and organise your group.
Perform and/or record it!

The Royal Family in the news

It is well known that Royalty can have a strange effect on those who come into contact with it.

Alexander Chancellor

1 An NOP survey in March 1986 revealed this information.
   Do you agree?

   The media pay far too much attention to the Royal Family.

Definitely agree	Tend to agree	Neither	Tend to disagree	Definitely disagree	Don't know
47%	26%	4%	14%	8%	1%

2 Events which for ordinary people would not be newsworthy are
   covered. In March 1986 Prince Charles was slightly injured in
   his home in Gloucestershire. Talk about what these two reports
   of the same incident tell us about:
   a) the Royal Family and newspapers
   b) different styles of coverage
   c) what the public 'likes' to hear.

CHARLES HURT

Prince Charles broke his
left index finger with a
hammer and cut himself
yesterday while planting
trees at his Gloucestershire
home, High Grove. The
wound was stitched and the
bone set at Princess
Margaret Hospital,
Swindon.

The Observer   23.3.1986

Charles in hospital car dash

by JOHN VINCENT

PRINCE CHARLES was rushed to hospital last
night suffering from a finger injury.

He was spending the weekend with Princess Diana at his Gloucestershire home, Highgrove House, when he had an accident in the garden.

He was taken to Princess Margaret Hospital in Swindon, Wiltshire.

A Buckingham Palace spokesman said:
'The Prince was planting a tree in his garden
and was putting in a stake.

'He missed with the hammer and hit himself. He has a broken bone in the index finger on
his left hand and it is badly lacerated.'

He added: 'He was taken first to Tetbury
Cottage Hospital, but there was no doctor there
able to treat him.'

The Prince had stitches put in his wound
and left the hospital with his arm in a sling.

'He was a perfect patient,' said one of the
nurses.

The Sunday Express   23.3.1986

3 In March 1986 *The Sunday Telegraph* devoted several paragraphs to considering why it was bothering to cover the engagement of Prince Andrew and Sarah Ferguson in such detail. Brainstorm all the reasons you can think of for Royalty being so widely covered in newspapers, especially at times of births, engagements and weddings. Put them into an order of importance.

WHY is this important page today given over entirely to articles about the engagement of Prince Andrew and Miss Sarah Ferguson? There is only one honest answer to this question. It is that we, like the rest of Fleet Street and everybody else in the media are labouring under the assumption that there is at present nothing else in the world of such consuming interest to the British public.

This is what everybody wants to read about, we have decided. Newspapers at the quality end of the market may scoff at the excesses of the popular press, but they do not argue with its priorities. All of Fleet Street is united in its judgment: the Andrew and Sarah story is a winner, one of which the people of Britain – who perforce include you, the readers of *The Sunday Telegraph* – cannot have enough.

A question arises. Are we right, or are we mad? If we are right, are you then mad? Or are we all equally mad? To talk of madness in this context is not entirely inappropriate for it is well known that Royalty can have a very strange effect on those who come into contact with it. Seasoned men of Fleet Street have been known to panic and try to curtsey to the Queen.

The Sunday Telegraph   23.3.1986

4 After the wedding of the Duke and Duchess of York these were some of the headlines. Certain different styles of coverage are evident. Try and describe them and decide on any appropriate categories.

Worldwide audience of 500 million applauds the finale

Prince Andrew and Miss Sarah Ferguson were married yesterday in an act of pure theatre which included its full complement of stunning costume, dramatic tension, the unravelling of oft-suspected plots, a single fluffed line, and a finale which gave immense satisfaction to a worldwide audience of 500 million.

The Times

Demon Prince has family in fits with fooling

THERE were **30,000** flowers in the Abbey along with history's most blooming Royal bride. But it was Sweet William's big day. The four-year-old future king blossomed wickedly. He stuck out his tongue, like a surplus red rose at the blushing bridesmaids.

Daily Express

What Fergie told her Andy in the Abbey

FUN-LOVING Fergie swept down the aisle of Westminster Abbey, took her place beside Prince Andrew and whispered ... "I've forgotten to pack my toothbrush."

The Sun

THE KISS

Presenting environmental issues

Are people poor because there are too many of them or are there many because there is widespread poverty?

Dave Hicks

1   Which of these issues do you consider to be important? Add your own to the chart if you prefer.

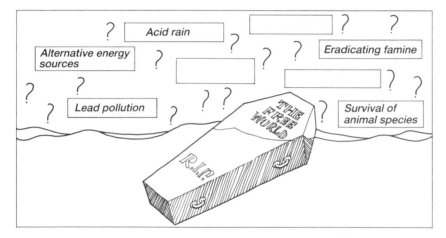

Acid rain

Alternative energy sources

Eradicating famine

Lead pollution

THE FREE WORLD

R.I.P.

Survival of animal species

2   Using some or all of these pictures prepare the newspaper article that you would like to see accompanying each one.

3   You will need to research your chosen subject. You will need to choose your language carefully being aware of what you are *implying* all the time.

4   Present your findings as a prepared talk to a small group.

5   Collect any articles you can find on these and related issues. In the light of the previous units discuss how they present environmental matters.

EXTENSION ACTIVITIES

This section is intended to develop ideas
introduced in Units 1 to 5.

A problem-solving activity

A man is found in the middle of the desert. He
has hanged himself from a tree. The tree is
perfectly smooth and offers no hand holds
below the branch from which he is hanging.
Therefore he could not have climbed up it.
Nor could he have reached it from the ground.
Not far away a vehicle is parked. There is one
set of footprints leading from the vehicle to
the tree; these footprints match the markings
on the soles of the shoes of the dead man.
There are no other marks. There is nothing in
the vehicle which he could have used to help
him reach the high branch. How did he do it?

*You probably know the answer. He brought
blocks of ice in the vehicle which he stood on
and which melted away afterwards.*

There are lots more riddles like this. For
example, there's the one about the man who
gets off a train in a big city, searches various
public places: airports, bars, restaurants, and
finally he finds the person he is looking for. It
is a man of similar colouring, age and size to
himself. He offers the man fifty thousand
pounds for his right arm. The other man,
being poor, agrees. The first man makes the
arrangements and the arm is amputated. When
the arm has been cut off the first man takes it,
puts it in a parcel and sends it to another city
where it is received by five other men, who
unwrap it, examine it and then, satisfied,
dispose of it. What is it all about?

Puzzling it out

The way to puzzle out these riddles is by asking questions to which the riddle has to answer yes or no. In the example above a good question to start with would have been: Does the first man know the men who received the arm? The answer would have been yes. Then you could have tried to discover exactly how he came to know them. You might eventually have discovered that he was a surgeon who had been shipwrecked with the other five men and that when the food had run out he had proposed that they each cut off an arm one by one to serve as food until help arrived; you might also have found out that he, as the surgeon performing the operations, needed both arms and so the others had made him agree that, if they were rescued, he would then cut off his own arm and send it to them as proof that he had kept his side of the bargain.

Not very likely, of course. But the more unlikely the story, the more fun it is to guess. Of course they don't all have to be that complicated. Here's a much simpler one:

Romeo and Juliet are both lying dead on the floor surrounded by water and broken glass. What's the explanation? Of course Romeo is a cat and Juliet a goldfish. You can work out for yourself how it happened.

Think up your own riddles and see if the others can guess them.

1   Sit down and think. Work out your riddle carefully so there are no flaws. The best way is to start from the end and work backwards.

2   Break up into groups of four. Each member of the group must put her/his riddle to the others, taking it in turns.

Gogs

Fortune telling: a planning activity

> If you can look into the seeds of time and say which grain will grow and which will not, speak then to me.
>
> *Shakespeare*

Have you ever wanted to have your fortune told? Or to tell someone else's fortune? Well now's your chance. Here is a simple method of consulting the cards. Please note that this is an exercise only. No one expects you to take fortune telling seriously.

1   **Either** take an ordinary deck of playing cards and select the ace, two, three and four of each suit, discarding the others; **or** cut out sixteen pieces of card and label them 1H to 4H (for hearts), 1C to 4C (for clubs) etc.

2   You may either ask the cards a question yourself or read the cards for someone else. The person seeking an answer should shuffle the cards, thinking all the time about the question s/he wants answered. The question should be as simple and straightforward as possible. For example: Don't ask, 'Will I pass my exam or won't I?' Just ask 'Will I pass my exam?'

3   When the person asking the question is ready, s/he should deal out seven cards, face downwards, in the pattern shown below.

How to lay out a reading

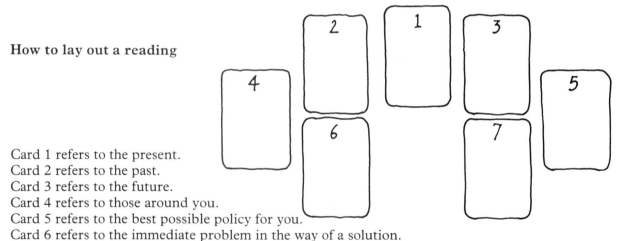

Card 1 refers to the present.
Card 2 refers to the past.
Card 3 refers to the future.
Card 4 refers to those around you.
Card 5 refers to the best possible policy for you.
Card 6 refers to the immediate problem in the way of a solution.
Card 7 refers to the probable final result.

4   Here are the meanings of the various cards:

	Clubs	Hearts	Diamonds	Spades
1	Ending	Beginning	Helping	Hindering
2	Failing	Succeeding	Wealth	Shame
3	Difficulty	Ease	Liking	Dislike
4	Trouble	Pleasure	Rest	Sorrow

Interpreting the cards

You have to decide what they mean. It isn't always obvious. For example, take the question about your exam. Your second card turned up might be the four of hearts: pleasure. At first that seems to make no sense at all. The exam was not a pleasure. But maybe the cards are suggesting that you enjoyed yourself too much when you should have been revising!

5 Once you have got a bit of practice you can try it the difficult way. Answer a friend's question using the cards but without knowing what the question is until afterwards. Of course your partner must be helpful and answer your questions or suggestions without misleading you.

6 Do you think there is anything in fortune telling? A lot of people do think so. The eminent psychiatrist, Karl Jung, developed a theory to explain it. He called this theory *synchronicity* – the theory of meaningful coincidences. One of his students put it like this:

> 'If an aircraft crashes before my eyes as I am blowing my nose, this is a coincidence of events that has no meaning. But if I bought a blue frock, and, by mistake, the shop delivered a black one on the day one of my near relatives died, this would be a meaningful coincidence.'

Have you ever experienced any meaningful coincidences in your life? Talk about them.

7 Another way of explaining 'synchronicity' is to say that everything in the world is connected with everything else even if only indirectly. If I drop a banana skin in the High Street I may not see the person who slips on it three days later, but there is a connection between us. Astrologers say that not only is everything connected to everything else, but there is also a pattern running through it all. You can see the same pattern that is written in your life written in the stars. What do you think of this argument?

8 Do you ever read your horoscope in a paper or magazine? Do you ever take any notice of it? Be honest! What is someone with your birth sign supposed to be like? Do you fit the description?

9 Horoscopes are always very general so that different people can read different things into them. They say things like: 'There will be opportunities to break new ground and enjoy new experiences.' Write your own horoscopes for other people in the group. See if they come true tomorrow!

Role-play activities

In the following role-play exercises you have to work **in pairs** to build up conversations of the kind which you can enact before the rest of the class at a later stage.

If music be the food of love

1 a) You work in a supermarket, not because you like it but because you get paid for it. It's not something you see yourself doing for very long. You need the money to spend on your music. You play synthesizer, guitar and sing. You write your own songs. You are very talented – at least that's what you think. You have a rehearsal room booked every Friday night where you practise. It costs you money. Right now it's five o'clock on Friday; you should be on your way out of the door but the boss wants you to work late – a load of cans of pineapple slices have still got to be stacked on the shelves.

   b) You are the supermarket boss. You don't exactly love your job but you do it because you have a family to support and a mortgage to pay. You don't dislike this kid whom you've employed to stack the shelves but you think s/he is a dreamer. S/he is never going to get anywhere in this world by playing pop music. Sure some people make it, but how many? It's a dirty business, the pop world and a lot of people get hurt. Right now you've got a lot of things on your plate. One of them is five hundred tins of pineapple that need stacking. That's what the kid is employed to do. After all you can't pack up on the dot of five. If s/he doesn't want the job there's plenty out there who do.

The best days of your life

2 a) When you were at school there was one teacher you hated above all others, who made your life really difficult, who was always putting you down and making you feel small. It was only after you left school that you discovered that you weren't stupid, that you had a lot going for you. In fact you have made quite a success of your life. You are highly paid, you have friends, material things, you are happy. One day you bump into your old teacher. You tell her/him what you think of her/him. Don't just be abusive; tell her/him where s/he went wrong.

   b) You are the teacher. You don't mean to put anyone down but you see your job as a matter of control. If you don't control the class it gets out of hand and no-one learns anything. Maybe you do pick on people sometimes but they should be tough enough to withstand it. Pupils give you a hard time and laugh at you but you live with it. It doesn't seem to have done this person any harm anyway since s/he is such a big success now. S/he must have learned something at school. You have to be realistic in this life: schools are not perfect, they are geared towards groups of pupils, not individuals. That's life.

That's what friends are for

3 **a)** Your parents come from Ireland but you were born in this country. You don't exactly see yourself as Irish in the way that someone who was born over there does, but that is your culture. Some parts of it you dislike, some parts of it you're proud of. The same could be said of your feelings about this country. Your friends are from various cultures, some black and some white. At the moment you are particularly upset because you have just been listening to one of them telling a racist joke. Of course s/he doesn't see it like that. To her/him it's just a laugh. The joke is about a stupid Irishman. When s/he told the joke, s/he was surrounded by her/his classmates; now s/he and you are alone. This is your chance to tell her/him just how s/he has let you down, and why.

b) A joke is a joke. That's the way you see it. Everyone should have a sense of humour. You're not a racist but you like a laugh. You don't actually believe that all the Irish are stupid, otherwise you wouldn't bother with your friend. It's just one of those things that people make jokes up about, like mean Scotsmen or Jews. You think your friend is much too touchy on this subject. After all we all have to live together.

Selling yourself

4 **a)** You are not an ambitious person. A lot of people tell you you should be, like your parents, your teachers and now even your friend. S/he is really ambitious. S/he wants to go to university and become a barrister. That's all right for her/him. But it doesn't interest you. In fact it seems to you that ambition is exactly what's wrong with the world because it means putting yourself first. That's why people are starving in places like Africa: because people are so busy thinking about their own personal ambitions that they haven't got time to try and make this a fairer world. You like your friend a lot but you don't like the ambitious streak in her/him. It seems to you that it's just her/his parents pushing her/him into it. You want to see a bit of life first and then make up your mind who or what you want to be.

b) You like your friend a lot. S/he is easy-going. That's a nice quality but you don't think s/he does her/himself justice. S/he could make much more of an impression on people if s/he dressed better, made an effort. The trouble is s/he doesn't ever think about the future. You have to think about the future otherwise you'll just be a drifter. You don't want to be a drifter. Your friend seems to want to change the world, but to change the world you have to have power, otherwise nobody takes any notice of you. You've got to sell yourself. There's nothing wrong with that. There's nothing wrong with wanting a big salary, a nice house. Your friend talks about helping the starving. You can't help poor people by becoming one yourself.

For the next role-play activities, work **in threes**.

A girl's best friend

5 a) **As a young woman** growing up in this society one of the things that really infuriates you is sexism. You have seen it all your life, all around you – people telling you what girls should do, how they should behave, what they should wear, how they should react to boys; pictures of women used to sell everything from car exhausts to lager. In protest against this you went out with a can of spray paint and began writing a slogan on a poster displayed in your local high street. Unfortunately you got stopped by a policeman half way through your protest. He insisted on treating you as if you were a child, refused to listen to your arguments and, instead of arresting you, brought you home to your parents in the hope that they might be able 'to talk some sense into you'. Your parents are shocked. Try to convince them that you are right. Work hardest on your mother. Get her on your side.

b) **As the father** you are horrified. You always thought your daughter was a nice girl. You cannot understand why she should want to start acting like a hooligan. As for all this feminism she has started coming out with, you don't want to have it in the house. This is, after all, your name and the mortgage is paid from your salary. Your wife's wages as a part-time cashier only pay for the little extras, the luxuries. But without you there would be no new clothes and not much to eat. That's something that everybody seems to have forgotten. All this feminism is all very well, in theory, but where is it getting your daughter? In trouble with the police, so far. If she wants to be so independent, then why doesn't she leave school, get a job in an office and begin to contribute something to the family finances?

c) **As the mother** you are horrified also. You have always brought your daughter up to be a good girl and she always has been. Yes, you see what she means. A bit of feminism wouldn't do her father any harm. He's been laying down the law for the last thirty years. But he doesn't really mean it. He just gets hot under the collar. Come to think of it she's a bit like her father: gets worked up about things. What she needs to learn is to compromise. You can't change the world. You just have to make the best you can out of it. Anyway, getting into trouble with the police – that's not going to help, is it?

Boys will be boys

6 a) **You** like fashion. It interests you and you have a flair for it. **As a male**, however, you have been discouraged from taking this interest seriously. There are no fashion courses at your school. You want to leave school and go to technical college where you can learn to design clothes. Your parents shake their heads in disbelief when you tell them this. But it only makes you more determined. As far as you are concerned it is your life and you will live it in your own way. That's not the way your parents look at it of course. Your father thinks that designing clothes is a job for a woman. Your mother thinks that you should stay on at school and get as many exams as possible.

b) **As his father** you only have his own interests at heart. But, yes you do think that designing clothes is a job for a woman or at least, you don't think it's a proper job for your son. You want to be proud of him. How can you be proud of someone who designs clothes? If your friends at work knew what your son wanted to be they'd laugh their heads off. This obsession with clothes is just something that he's got from watching TV – all those pop stars dressed in ridiculous clothes, men who look like women. That's what he's going to turn out like if he's not careful. It's unhealthy.

c) **As the boy's mother** you only want what's best for him. You think he'll grow out of all this. It's just a fad. Then he'll be glad he stayed on at school. You don't see any harm in boys designing clothes but you can't see a lot of future in it either. What he wants is a steady job not some sort of dream. If he was a girl it would be different. Maybe it's not right but that's the way the world is. Girls can find employment in that field. But it's different for boys. He wants the world to take him seriously, doesn't he? His father's right about that. People will only laugh. You don't want anyone laughing at your son.

In the name of the law

Your school deals with problems of discipline and disputes between pupils by its own legal system. Serious cases, like the one below, are tried by a judge and jury with counsels for the prosecution and for the defence.

1 You are going to try one such case. First read the nature of the crime and what the Defendant (the person charged with the crime) had to say when arrested by the Head of Year.

Nature of the crime: The Defendant is charged with stealing a coat.

Time: Friday, 1.00 p.m.

Place: The school cloakroom, which is run by volunteers, who give out tickets in return for bags or coats.

Statement: I went to the cloakroom at lunchtime on Friday and discovered that I didn't have a ticket. I immediately thought that I must have lost my ticket. I explained this to the attendant, who asked me to describe my coat. S/he brought out several coats and I chose one identical to mine. It was only when I got home that I realised it wasn't mine. My coat was at the cleaners because of a big stain on the sleeve. I had forgotten this. Normally I wear my coat to school every day and leave it in the cloakroom. I intended to bring the coat back on Monday. I wore it to a disco on Saturday. I know I shouldn't have but there didn't seem any harm in it as I was going to bring it back on Monday. The owner of the coat, who was also at the disco, recognised it and reported me to the Head of Year on Monday morning before I had a chance to return it to the cloakroom, as I arrived a bit late to school.

---

2 These are the rules of the court:
   a) The Defendant is asked whether s/he pleads guilty or not guilty.
   b) The Prosecuting Counsel makes an opening speech.
   c) The Prosecuting Counsel calls witnesses and cross-examines them.
   d) Each Prosecution witness may also be cross-examined by Defence Counsel.
   e) Defence Counsel makes an opening speech.
   f) Defence Counsel calls witnesses and cross-examines them.
   g) Each Defence witness may also be cross-examined by Prosecuting Counsel.
   h) Prosecuting Counsel makes a summing-up speech.
   i) Defence Counsel makes a summing-up speech.
   j) Jury retires to consider verdict.
   k) Jury gives verdict.

Special Notes

★ The Defendant is innocent until proved guilty.
★ Counsels may do all in their power to cast doubt on witnesses.
★ Counsels may object to unfair questioning.

3 Break up into **groups of five**. The teacher will call some groups
   A and some groups **B**.

A groups

You have to prepare the following roles. All members must help with all roles:

The Defendant

Counsel for the Defence
You have to work out your speeches and your questions.

1st Defence Witness
You have known the defendant since Primary School. Because of an incident that happened about a year ago, you have very good reason to believe the Defendant to be totally honest. It was you who spilled the coffee on the Defendant's coat and you can clearly remember her/his reaction at the time. You were not in school on Friday but you did see the Defendant on Sunday in a café with several other people. Did you notice whether s/he was wearing the coat or not? What did you talk about?

2nd Defence Witness
You have known the Defendant well only since the beginning of this year. You transferred to this school from another. You went to the cloakroom with her/him on Friday and to the Disco on Saturday. You often go out with the Defendant who seems to have plenty of money to spend on clothes and records. Did s/he mention anything about the coat on Saturday?

3rd Defence Witness
You arrived late on Monday morning with the Defendant. You are not a particular friend of the Defendant though you have known her/him since you both joined this school. Why were you both late?

B groups

You have to prepare the following roles. All members must help with all roles:

Counsel for the Prosecution
You have to work out your speeches and your questions.

1st Prosecution Witness
The owner of the coat. You know the Defendant well and you consider her/him to be dishonest. Why? Why did you not speak to her/him at the disco?

2nd Prosecution Witness
The cloakroom attendant. You do not know the Defendant at all. Is your version of events any different to the statement made by the Defendant?

3rd Prosecution Witness
You were in a café where you saw the Defendant on Sunday. You did not speak to her/him because you do not like each other. Why? But you could overhear her/his conversation. What did s/he say? Did you notice whether s/he was wearing the coat?

4th Prosecution Witness
The Head of Year. What did the Defendant say and how did s/he react when arrested on Monday morning? What else do you know about her/his attendance, punctuality and general record of behaviour which might have a bearing on this case?

4 The teacher picks one of the A groups and one of the B groups. The others act as the jury. The Jury must elect a Chairperson to count their votes and give their verdict. One member might like to be the Clerk of the Court, whose job it is to ask the Defendant what her/his plea is, and to swear in each witness. The teacher acts as judge.

A structured talking activity

To paint the portrait of a bird

First paint a cage
with an open door
then paint
something pretty
something simple
something beautiful
something useful ...
for the bird
then place the canvas against a tree
in a garden
in a wood
or in a forest
hide behind the tree
without speaking
without moving ...
Sometimes the bird comes quickly
but he can just as well spend long years
before deciding
Don't get discouraged
wait
wait years if necessary
the swiftness or slowness of the coming
of the bird having no rapport
with the success of the picture

When the bird comes
if he comes
observe the most profound silence
wait till the bird enters the cage
and when he has entered
gently close the door with a brush
then
paint out all the bars one by one
taking care not to touch any of the feathers of the bird
Then paint the portrait of the tree
choosing the most beautiful of its branches
for the bird
paint also the green foliage and the wind's freshness
the dust of the sun
and the noise of insects in the summer heat
and then wait for the bird to decide to sing
If the bird doesn't sing
it's a bad sign
a sign that the painting is bad
but if he sings it's a good sign
a sign that you can sign
so then so very gently you pull out
one of the feathers of the bird
and you write your name in a corner of the picture.

Jaques Prévert

1 Read the poem. In some ways it is similar to the story of Nasrudin we looked at in *A Programmed Discussion* on page 32. You might like to investigate it in a similar way but this time using a computer to help you. **Working in pairs**, write your own programs.

2 First decide what areas in the poem you want to investigate. For example, you might decide that the bird described is not just an ordinary bird but a symbol for something else, so some of your questions would concentrate on what the something could be.

3 When you have decided what questions you want to consider you will need to tell the computer to ask them. But first tell it how to recognise the answers 'yes' and 'no'. Like this:

> 10. LET A\$ = 'Yes'
> 20. LET B\$ = 'No'

4 Now you are ready to ask the computer to print the questions. Like this:

> 30. PRINT 'This poem has a hidden meaning. Do you think it has something to do with the bird?' Yes/no.

5 Make a space in your program for the answer that you or your partner will give. Like this:

> 40. INPUT C\$

6 Instruct the computer either to move on to the next stage of the program or to pause to allow discussion. To simply move on write:

> 50. IF C\$ = A\$ THEN GOTO 80

Your next question will appear at 80. At 60 and 70 you can create a discussion activity. Like this:

> 60. PRINT 'On paper make a list of your reasons for disagreeing. When you have finished type in yes.'
> 70. INPUT D\$

7 Clearly it is possible to create very involved programs using the IF . . . THEN facility. But it is never a good idea to make things more complicated than they need to be.

8 Writing even the smallest program takes a lot of working out and a certain amount of trial and error. Good luck.

Note: the instructions printed above may need modifying to suit the particular computer you are using.

Developing an argument

The smoker's view

Sir,

Your newspaper, along with the media, continues to harass
smokers who already pay very highly for their pleasures,
in many cases their only pleasure.

Even in the worst of criminal cases the lawyers are able to
say something in defence of the accused, so I will attempt to
do just that, since no-one else will give us a hearing.

I strongly object to motorists in particular lecturing me on
my smoking habits, when they collectively make living in our
cities a very dangerous occupation. Since when did a smoker
pollute the whole of our atmosphere with fumes, as does the
motorist with his polluted fumes with a heavy content of lead
which according to the medical profession is harmful to us
all and, in particular, the mental danger of children living
in congested areas?

I feel in particular that the non-smoking motorist should
think very carefully before attacking those of us who pay
so much in taxes for our habit.

It is also worth mentioning the fact that if the anti-
smoking campaign is successful the complainants will have
a very heavy tax burden to pay.

Yours,

Alan Johns

Alan Johns,
Cardiff,
Wales.

In pairs, write a joint letter to a newspaper in which you
present a difficult argument of your own choice.

Talking about issues

What being Black and British means to me

I can never think of myself as being Black and British at the same time. It's my opinion that these two facts are somewhat opposite each other, what I mean is how can you be British if you are Black?

I always thought of myself as being not British but a West Indian who happened to be born in Britain. I know that I was born in Britain, I am supposed to be classed as British citizen but I never refer to myself as being British among my fellow black people. Personally this sounds like a sell-out to my history.

However, this does not mean that I will allow any white person to tell me that I should be sent back where I came from or any similar phrase. In those situations I point out clearly to them that I was born here and have as much entitlement to remain here as they do. No person has the right to tell me where I should or should not be.

Jeanette Elliott, aged 17

I was fortunate enough to go to a school where I was encouraged to and wanted to work hard. I also received a lot of support from my parents. However, many parents believe by going to school that education can be 'rubbed' onto their children. This is an absolute fallacy. The most important feature is a good teacher/pupil, parent/school relationship. This is important for any child to do well. Teachers will often encourage blacks to do well in sports which they assume is their natural forte; but it seems the same cannot be said of the classroom.

Being black does have its advantages. It is a sense of identification. Something which one should be proud to have. We should feel different, yes even superior to those around us. I felt at school that although I am part of the class I am in a sense, different. Whatever others can do I should try to do at least as well. Again, parents can help their children. All of us go through periods when we are depressed or unhappy, especially at school. Instead of just telling off, parents should try and understand. They must remember that the education system in Britain is different from back home.

M. Hutchinson, aged 19

1 What impression do you get of what it is like to be black and British in the 1980s?

2 Talk about any experiences you have which involve feeling different from other people.

More issues: patriotism

1 Compare these two extracts from well-known patriotic songs.

Rule Britannia

> When Britain first, at heaven's command,
> Arose from out the azure main
> This was the charter of the land
> And guardian angels sung this strain:
>   'Rule, Britannia, rule the waves;
>   Britons never will be slaves.'

God Save Ireland

> High upon the gallows tree swung the noble-hearted three
> By the vengeful tyrant stricken in their bloom;
> But they met him face to face with the spirit of their race,
> And they went with souls undaunted to their doom.
>   'God save Ireland' said the heroes. 'God save Ireland
>   said they all;
>   'Whether on the scaffold high or the battle-field we die,
>   Oh what matter when for Erin★ dear we fall.'

★Erin – poetic name for Ireland.

2 Make a list of the differences between these two extracts and of the similarities.

3 In the second song why do you think the three were hung? Why does the writer describe them as 'noble-hearted'?

4 What do the words 'this was the charter of the land' mean in the first song? What is the effect of saying 'Guardian angels sung this strain'?

5 Do you think that patriotism is still important today? How important is it to you?

6 What are the negative aspects of patriotism?

7 Is it possible to be patriotic without being hostile towards other countries or races?

8 List three reasons why these songs should be banned.

9 List three reasons why these songs should be taught to children in primary schools.

10 Make up your own patriotic song:
   a) for the country you were born in
      or
   b) for an imaginary country
      or
   c) for the country of your choice.

11 How important is patriotism in public figures? Give a rating from 1 to 5 for the importance of patriotism among the following:
   a) the Prime Minister
   b) a pop star
   c) the head of the civil service
   d) the Archbishop of Canterbury
   e) the head of a large company
   f) a teacher.

One liners

The following scenarios are each written for two people though others may join in if they wish. Turn them into conversations that tell a story.

Place: A street
First line: My God, I didn't expect to see you here!
Known facts: They are sisters, brothers or sister/brother.

Place: A funeral
First line: I know I shouldn't say it but I'm glad he's dead.
Known facts: They are not related.

Place: A car
First line: We were lucky to get out of there alive.
Known facts: None.

Place: The wings of a stage
First line: I'm never going through that again!
Known facts: They are both performers.

Place: An airport
First line: It's in this box.
Known facts: They are not terrorists.

Place: A school
First line: Is she in the building?
Known facts: They are both teachers.

Place:	A school
First line:	Stop I need to talk to you.
Known facts:	They are both students.

Place:	A room
First line:	My parents sent you, didn't they?
Known facts:	They are friends.

Place:	A hospital
First line:	Only another week to go.
Known facts:	They are not doctors.

Place:	A pub
First line:	I thought I'd find you here.
Known facts:	Both run market stalls.

Place:	A boat
First line:	Can you swim?
Known facts:	They dislike each other.

Place:	An aeroplane
First line:	You know what to do when we get off.
Known facts:	They do not trust each other.

Place:	A kitchen
First line:	Look it's in the paper.
Known facts:	They have not had much sleep recently.

Place:	An old house
First line:	This is the room but it's been changed.
Known facts:	The house does not belong to either of them.

Place:	An office
First line:	This is where I work.
Known facts:	One of them is frightened.

A working-with-stories activity

The examination

At five minutes to eleven, they called the name of Jordan.

'Good luck, son,' his father said, without looking at him. 'I'll call for you when the test is over.'

Dickie walked to the door and turned the handle. The room inside was dim, and he could hardly make out the features of the grey-tunicked attendant who greeted him.

'Sit down,' the man said softly. He indicated a high stool beside his desk. 'Your name's Richard Jordan?'

'Yes, sir.'

'Your classification number is 600–115. Drink this, Richard.'

He lifted a plastic cup from the desk and handed it to the boy. The liquid inside it had the consistency of buttermilk and tasted vaguely of peppermint. Dickie downed it, and handed the man the empty cup.

He sat in silence, feeling drowsy, while the man wrote busily on a sheet of paper. Then the attendant looked at his watch, and rose to stand only inches from Dickie's face. He unclipped a penlike object from the pocket of his tunic and flashed a tiny light into the boy's eyes.

'All right,' he said. 'Come with me, Richard.'

He led Dickie to the end of the room, where a single wooden armchair faced a multi-dialled computing machine. There was a microphone on the left arm of the chair, and when the boy sat down, he found its pinpoint head conveniently at his mouth.

'Now just relax, Richard. You'll be asked some questions, and you think them over carefully. Then give your answers into the microphone. The machine will take care of the rest.'

'Yes, sir,'

'I'll leave you alone now. Whenever you want to start, just say "ready" into the microphone.'

'Yes, sir.'

The man squeezed his shoulder, and left.

Dickie said, 'Ready.'

Lights appeared on the machine, and a mechanism whirred. A voice said:

'Complete this sequence. One, four, seven, ten . . .'

     ★   ★   ★   ★   ★   ★

Mr and Mrs Jordan were in the living room, not speaking, not even speculating.

It was almost four o'clock when the telephone rang. The woman tried to reach it first, but her husband was quicker.

'Mr Jordan?'

The voice was clipped; a brisk, official voice.

'Yes, speaking.'

'This is the Government Educational Service. Your son, Richard M. Jordan, Classification 600–115, has completed the Government examination. We regret to inform you that his intelligence quotient has exceeded the Government regulation, according to Rule 84, Section 5, of the New Code.'

Across the room, the woman cried out, knowing nothing except the emotion she read on her husband's face.

'You may specify by telephone,' the voice droned on, 'whether you wish his body interred by the Government or would you prefer a private burial place? The fee for Government burial is ten dollars.'

From *Examination Day* by Henry Slesar

1   What was going to happen to Richard Jordan?

2   What possible reasons can you think up for this state of affairs?

3   Discuss the kind of world this story seems to be describing.

4   If you had to design an intelligence test containing only ten questions, what would they be?

5   Try them out on a friend.

6   Continue this story *orally*, possibly taking it in turns.

Formal debates

How to have a formal debate

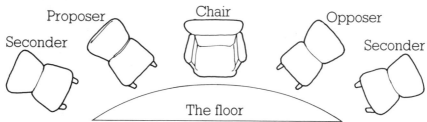

Proposer Chair Opposer

Seconder Seconder

The floor

Before the debate

1   Agree on a motion (the name given to the subject of the debate).

2   Elect four principal speakers and a chairperson.

3   Prepare speeches whether you are a main speaker or just going to contribute from the floor.

The debate

4   The motion is introduced by the chairperson.

5   The proposer speaks *for* the motion.

6   The opposer speaks *against* the motion.

7   The two seconders speak, normally for slightly less time than the proposer and the opposer.

8   The chairperson then invites contributions to the debate from the audience (the 'floor'). These may be prepared views or responses to the speeches already heard.

9   The opposer sums up the arguments *against* the motion.

10   The proposer concludes the case *for* the motion.

The vote

11   The chairperson takes a vote. This includes:
    a) those for the motion
    b) those against the motion and
    c) abstentions (those who don't wish to vote either way).

12   The result is then formally given out and the debate closed.

This format can be varied to suit the needs of those taking part.

A balloon debate

One particularly famous 'debate' involves speakers in a less formal kind of discussion.

The situation

You are in a balloon travelling over high mountains when disaster strikes. The balloon begins to lose height. You have already thrown out all available ballast. You are left with no alternative other than choosing one member of your group to be jettisoned as ballast. You decide that each person in the group will have to make a speech arguing his or her right to stay in the balloon.

How to have a balloon debate

1   You can either limit numbers or involve the whole class.

2   Each person has a time-limit for speaking e.g. 3 minutes.

3   A vote is taken at the end on the strength of the speeches.

You can either use your own characters or take on roles from fiction or history

Other possible topics for debate

This house believes that . . .

1   nobody should be allowed to earn more than £20,000 a year

2   Britain should get rid of all its nuclear weapons

3   all children should be taught to write left-handedly

4   everybody should carry identity papers

5   fashion and pop music should be banned

6   private education should be illegal

7   the Royal Family should be abolished

8   rapists should be treated as murderers

9   capital punishment should be re-introduced

10   national service should be re-introduced.

Important discussions world-wide

Decide where these 'debates' are taking place.

[Answers on page 90.]

1

2

4

3

5

6

7

8

Answers

Page 17 *A murder mystery*

The murderer was Marie Delworth. She hid in Ford's bathroom when the butler arrived. Mark Members knew it wasn't Declan O'Rourke when he shook hands – O'Rourke's arthritis would not have allowed him to leave bruises on someone's throat.

Page 19 *Pensioner in bank raid (contd.)*

'The Recorder of London, Sir James Miskin QC, said that the raid had been doomed from the start but had still led to a lot of trouble. He added that before the offence Mrs Barlow had led a 'socially splendid and responsible' life and had been too proud to ask for help with her finances (which have since been resolved by the sale of her cottage). Sentencing her to nine months' imprisonment, suspended for a year, he warned her not to do anything idiotic again.

Mrs Barlow thanked him and left the court to have a glass of Scotch and describe how she had planned a 'kind and gentle' raid in contrast to the ones she saw on television

'I must have had a brainstorm. I'm normally a very placid and timid person,' she said. 'Mercifully, everyone has been very kind and understanding and I've promised not to break the law again.''

Page 43 *Dateline*

1 = 1960–1980		4 = 1750–1850	
2 = 1900–1920		5 = 1930–1950	
3 = 1600–1650			

Page 43 *Missing words*

1	Teachers	4	Dump	7	brains	10	teachers
2	glass	5	special	8	prospects	
3	Cigarettes	6	school	9	blank	

Page 48 *Not now Bernard*

The correct order is:
A, G, H, L, M, P, B, O, N, K, C, J, I, D, F, E, Q

Page 61 *Television advertisements*

breath-testing devices etc, marriage agencies, fortune tellers etc., undertakers, betting activities, cigarettes, private investigation agencies, contraceptives, smoking cures, hair clinics, pregnancy testing services and others

Pages 88–89 1 A college. 2 South Africa. 3 A party conference. 4 An office. 5 A Church of England synod. 6 Ethiopia. 7 A suffragette rally in Trafalgar Square in 1908. 8 The United Nations.

To the student

How to record your progress in oral work

- Each time your work in English involves talking or listening, record the date on the record sheets on pages 92/93.

- As you begin to understand what a particular skill involves, tick under one of the three faces to indicate how confident you feel about it.

☺   if you feel confident you can do it well

☺   if you feel you can do this reasonably well

☹   if you feel you need more help and practice

- Add comments of your own next to individual skills. These should help you record your reactions to particular areas of oral work.

Example

I can talk about poems	Dates			Tick here			Comment
	13/2	7/5	9/3	☺	☺✓	☹	*I like poems but don't always know what to say about them.*

In this example you might be able to get help from your teacher or another student.

Remember

1   Don't expect to be able to fill all of the record sheet in: these skills take much time and practice before being mastered.

2   Don't expect your sheet to be the same as anyone else's.

3   Don't assume you have mastered a skill just because you have practised it a few times!

4   Use your record sheet as a means of recording your own progress and achievements.

Name

Skill	Dates recorded			Tick here			Student comment
				😊	😐	☹️	
I can analyse information							
brainstorm							
chair discussions							
change my mind after listening							
develop an argument							
explain myself clearly							
give my own opinions							
interview people							
justify what I say							
listen to others' opinions							
match my language to the situation							
organise my ideas							
persuade people to agree with me							
play imaginary roles							
predict from information given							

Name_____

Skill	Dates recorded			Tick here			Student comment
				☺	☺	☹	
I can put a list in suitable order							
report back on discussions							
share my ideas with others							
solve problems							
speak up in discussions							
stick to a simple, given role							
sum up what has been said							
take clear notes							
take decisions							
take part in a debate							
talk about diagrams							
talk about pictures							
talk about plays							
talk about poems							
talk about stories							

To the teacher

This sourcebook for oral work is designed to complement and where possible integrate with other work in English. It is *not* intended that oral and aural work should be seen as separate features of students' work in English.

In brief:

■ talking almost inevitably involves listening
■ the best oral work often grows out of work actually being undertaken and employs a variety of skills
■ talking and listening integrate naturally with reading and writing
■ it is important that students should experience a variety of different audiences, where possible *genuine* ones
■ it is particularly important to monitor progress in all forms of oral activity and record achievement

The book provides three main kinds of activity. This organisation necessarily presents some apparently discrete areas of oral activity. However this is only for ease of use and it is hoped that material will be freely adapted and interpreted.

The three activities are:

1 Starters
Shorter less involved stimulus material for pairs and small groups

2 Main units
Double pages of reasonably self-contained material for more detailed groupwork

3 Extension material
Varied material sometimes designed to link up with further work or to be adapted to fit work already being undertaken in English.

Skills checklist

Adopting different roles in a group
Analysing data
Brainstorming
Chairing discussion
Contributing to discussion
Developing an argument
Employing appropriate strategies
Explaining
Exploring responses to literature
Giving and listening to opinions
Having a formal debate
Interviewing
Justifying
Modifying a point of view
Organising ideas
Persuading
Playing everyday roles
Playing imaginary roles
Predicting
Prioritising
Reporting back on a discussion
Responding to visual material
Sharing ideas
Solving problems
Summarising
Taking decisions
Taking notes
Talking to different audiences
Using appropriate register of language

NB Key skills which may provide pointers to students' overall development are italicised. Page numbers are not provided for these as they will be being developed in most types of oral work.

Addresses

British Nuclear Forum
1 St Alban's St., London SW1Y 4SL

British Nuclear Fuels PLC
Information Services Directorate
Risley, Warrington, Cheshire WA3 6AS

Central Electricity Generating Board
Public Information Manager,
Sudbury House, 15 Newgate St.,
London EC1A 7AU

Friends Of The Earth Trust Ltd.,
377 City Road, London EC1V 1NA

Health Education Council
78 New Oxford St., London WC1A 1AH

Campaign For Press And Broadcasting Freedom
9 Poland St., London W1V 3DG

Commission For Racial Equality
Elliot House, Allington Street, London SW1

RSPCA
Education Officer
Causeway, Horsham, West Sussex RH12 1HG

Research Defence Society
Grosvenor Gardens House, Grosvenor Gardens,
London SW1 0BS

The Independent Broadcasting Authority
70 Brompton Rd., London SW3 1EY

Association for Smoking and Health
5/11 Mortimer Street, London W1

Acknowledgements

The publishers would like to thank the following for permission to use copyright material.

Douglas Adams: *The Hitch Hiker's Guide to the Galaxy.* Reprinted by permission of Pan Books.

Charles Causley: 'The Ballad of Charlotte Dymond' from *Collected Poems.* Reprinted by permission of David Higham Associates Ltd.

Roald Dahl: 'Cinderella' from *Revolting Rhymes.* Reprinted by permission of the author and Jonathan Cape Ltd.

Marjorie Darke: from *A Question of Courage* © 1975 by Marjorie Darke. Used by permission.

Jeanette Ellison and M Hutchinson: *What Being Black and British Means to Me* from Black Youth Annual Penmanship Awards 1980. Reprinted by permission of the Afro-Caribbean Education Resource Centre.

Charles Freeman: from *Terrorism.* Reprinted by permission of B T Batsford Ltd.

Alan Gilbey: *Disruptive Minority* first published as *Second Year Defeat* in *Bricklight* (ed. Chris Searle) and reprinted in *Standpoints* (ed. John Foster, Harrap 1983).

David McKee: from *Not now Bernard.* Reprinted by permission of Anderson Press Ltd.

Jacques Prévert: *To Paint the Portrait of a Bird* Copyright © 1947 by Les Editions du Point du Jour. Reprinted by permission of City Lights Books.

Henry Slesar: from 'Examination Day' in *The Playboy Book of Science Fiction and Fantasy.* Reprinted by permission of Henry Slesar and Campbell Thomson and McLaughlin Limited.

Biofotos, p.65 (top left); Building Magazine, p.65 (top left); Camera Press, pp.19 (bottom four), p.54 (top centre two), p.64 (right), p.65 (bottom right); Colorific! (Photo: David Turnley), p.57 (right); Camerapix Hutchinson, p.89 (centre left); Careers and Occupational Information Centre, p.88 (bottom right); Collins Publishers (from Judith Kerr *The Tiger who came to Tea*), p.58; Imperial War Museum, p.81 (all); ITN News Ltd, p.54 (top left); Mary Evans Picture Library, p.89 (centre right); Isobel Miller, p.8 (right); Rex Features, pp.19 (top), 57 (left), 88 (bottom left), 89 (top); Taylor Woodrow, p.65 (bottom left); John Twinning, p.8 (left); United Nations Information Centre (Photo: M. Tzovaras), p.89 (bottom); World Wildlife Fund (Photo: R. Mittermeir), p.64 (left).

Illustrations by Sue Heap, Marie-Hélène Jeeves, Susan Scott